between

fun talk about faith,
friends, & family

us
girls

between

fun talk about faith, friends, & family
by vicki courtney

us
girls

B&H
PUBLISHING GROUP

between

us girls:

fun talk about faith, friends, & family

Copyright © 2008 by Vicki Courtney
All rights reserved.
Printed in the United States of America
Published by B&H Publishing Group
Nashville, Tennessee

ISBN: 978-0-8054-4667-8

Dewey Decimal Classification: 305

Subject Heading: GIRLS \ CHRISTIAN LIFE

5 6 7 8 9 10   17 16 15 14 13

Cover Design: Emily Keafer for Anderson Design Group
Interior Design: Emily Keafer, Kristi Smith, and Amy Olert for Anderson Design Group

CHeCK ThiS Out!

Author's Web Sites

VickiCourtney.com: stay up to date with the latest information regarding Vicki's books, speaking engagements, or invite her to speak at your event.

Virtuousreality.com: an online magazine for middle and high school girls highlighting relevant articles, a blog feature, a prayer board, and artist of the month.

VirtueAlert.com: Vicki's blog geared to parents highlighting issues relevant in today's culture.

Other books by Vicki Courtney from B&H:

Between: A Girl's Guide to Life

Your Girl: Raising a Godly Daughter in an Ungodly World

Yada Yada: A Devotional Journal for Moms

More Than Just Talk: A Journal for Girls

The Virtuous Woman: Shattering the Superwoman Myth

Teen Virtue: Real Issues, Real Life . . . A Teen Girl's Survival Guide

TeenVirtue 2: A Teen Girl's Guide to Relationships

TeenVirtue Confidential: Your Questions About God, Guys, and Getting Older

Your Boy: Raising a Godly Son in an Ungodly World

table of contents

chapter 3
The Bible

chapter 4
FRiends, Family, and Others

chapter 5
Just for fun

about the Authors

Vicki Courtney is the founder of Virtuous Reality Ministries that hosts virtuousreality.com, an online magazine for teen girls. She is also a speaker and best-selling author of many books for parents, teen girls, and tween girls. She lives in Austin, Texas, with her husband, Keith, their three children, and two pint-size Yorkies. In her spare time she loves to spend time with her family at their lake house and watch her kids tube behind the boat. Sometimes her dogs join them on the boat in their tiny lifejackets! For more information about Vicki and to see pictures of her family (and yes, her dogs!) go to: www.vickicourtney.com. Be sure to tell your mom about Vicki's blog where she talks about lots of "mom stuff"!

Kids: Ryan (20), Paige (18), and Hayden (15)

Pets: Lexie Grace and Scout

Weird talent: I can ride a unicycle!

I'm afraid of: getting trapped in an elevator or any small space—I'm very claustrophobic!

Favorite Bible verse: 2 Corinthians 5:17 (first Bible verse I memorized after becoming a Christian)

Biggest pet peeve: when people talk on their cell phones in public restrooms! What's up with that?

Favorite candy: SweetTarts all the way!

Something I can't live without: Diet Dr. Pepper

Susie Davis is an author and speaker. She is the founder of Susie Davis Ministries, which is an event, resource, and Web-based ministry. Her book bio includes *The Time of Your Life* and *Loving Your Man without Losing Your Mind.* She is currently writing a book to help moms everywhere learn how to love their teenage kids without going crazy. In her free time, Susie rides her horse Molly Brown (a Thoroughbred bay) or throws the ball for her cat Madeleine (a black and white stray). But most days she spends trying to quiet down her two Labs, Mike and Mary Spoon. Susie and her husband, Will Davis Jr., live in Austin, Texas, with their three children: Will III, Emily, and Sara. For more information, visit www.susiedavisministries.com.

Kids: Will III (21), Emily (18), and Sara (14)

Weird family facts: all our pets' names begin with "m" including Mango our twelve-year-old parakeet

Scariest thing I've done: climbed Long's Peak (elevation 14,259 ft) with my husband

Favorite Gospel in the Bible: Mark

Something I can't live without: McDonald's coffee (four creams/no sugar)

Favorite snack food: Ak-mak sesame crackers and Honey-crisp apples

Julie Ferwerda is a freelance writer who lives somewhere in the treacherous snow-covered jungles of Wyoming with her husband and two wacky teenagers, Danielle and Jessica. She has contributed to Thomas Nelson *Revolve Biblezines for Teen Girls* and *Revolve Devotional Bible* as well as written for *Brio* magazine. She is currently working on a book about kids all over the world who are changing their cultures and countries for Christ. For more info about her writing and family life, go to www.JulieFerwerda.com.

Kids: Danielle (16) and Jessica (13)

Pets: two cats: Pepe Le Pew & Morty

Weird fact: I don't need to use deodorant (seriously)

Weird talent: I can reach the end of my nose with my tongue

I'm afraid of: waking up with a rattlesnake trying to get warm in my sleeping bag while camping

Favorite Bible verse: Hekeziah 3:15 (be sure to look it up!)

Biggest pet peeve: somebody putting their cold hands on my warm body in winter

Favorite ice cream flavor: no-calorie super creamy fudge-almond-cake batter-caramel-coconut swirl (I think they make it in heaven!)

Susan Jones is the director for special events at Prestonwood Christian Academy in Plano, Texas. She is the former program director for Virtuous Reality Ministries and has contributed to *Between: A Girl's Guide to Life* and *Teen Virtue Confidential*, both by Vicki Courtney. Her heart beats fast for any "outdoorsy" activity, Labrador retrievers and homemade ice cream with brownies. But, her heart beats faster when she studies, teaches, and writes about God and his Word! (She's a bit of a spaz about it.)

Kids: Hopefully someday!

Something I can't live without: pizza

Coolest place I've been: Italy

Coolest thing I've done: hiked Mount Sinai (like Moses)

Favorite books of the Bible: Daniel, James, and Psalms

Weird fact: I put all my cereal, crackers, and chips in the refrigerator. (They never get stale!)

INTRODUCTION

I **LOVE to Talk.** In fact, when I was your age, I got in trouble quite a bit in school for talking too much. In eighth grade my Science teacher got so fed up with me turning around to talk with my friend, who sat in the desk behind me, that he gave me a choice one day: detention after school or I could stand up in front of the whole class and do a cheer (I was a cheerleader). Duh, that one was a no-brainer! "Two-bit, four-bits, six-bits, a dollar; all for photosynthesis stand up and holler!" I knew there was no way I could survive an hour of stone-cold silence in detention. You would think I would learn my lesson after suffering from that sort of public humiliation but, noooooooooo. I was busted a month later in math class for passing a note to my best friend. Mrs. Cooper intercepted the note and yeah, you guessed it, she read it out loud to the class. I'm not sure what was more embarrassing: saying Mrs. Cooper was the meanest teacher ever or confessing my crush on a boy that unfortunately was sitting right there in class. Ugh.

I've always heard that girls have more words that they need to get out each day than the guys. And speaking of that, have you ever noticed how short guys' conversations are?

"Hey."

"Hey."

"You going to the game tonight?"

"Yeah."

"Me too."

"Awesome."

"See ya there."

They always get right to the point. Girls, on the other hand, just like talking for the sake of talking. We're all about the details. In this issue of *Between Us Girls*, we let girls your age do the talking. When we were writing it, we did a survey and asked girls your age all kinds of questions about God, family, friends, and other random stuff. Ever wonder if other girls your age share the same favorite Bible verse as you? Or maybe they want to do the same thing you do when you grow up. We also asked them some fun questions like what their most embarrassing moment was or the craziest pet name they've ever heard. I think you'll enjoy reading their answers and it'll be even more fun if you gather around with your friends and share your answers. Just one suggestion. Don't buzz about it in Science class!

–Vicki Courtney

Chapter 1:
Me
Myself
& i

the SECRET to LASTING HAPPINESS

by Susie Davis

Wouldn't it be great to feel happy all the time?

When I was little, I remember thinking that if I could be happy all the time, my life would be just perfect. In fourth grade I thought that if only I could do a back handspring, I would be happy.

In fifth grade I imagined that getting a lead role in the school play would fill me with happiness. And by sixth grade, I just knew that if one certain boy liked me back— I would be the happiest girl in the whole world.

Now even though some of those things did happen to me when I was in grade school, the happy meter in my life didn't always register full. For instance, when I finally found out that one certain boy liked me back (which I begged God for and told him it would make me oh so happy forever!), it didn't mean that I stayed happy. Boys are fun, of course, but it's not enough to keep a girl waking up every day saying, "Oh my goodness! I am the luckiest person alive because Jason likes me! I'm really happy and I'll be happy forever!" No, that's kinda crazy and you probably realize that, but I wonder . . . when you think of what will make you happy, are you able to see your crazy thought patterns? It is always harder to think clearly about your own life with things like these.

Try something. Write down ten things that you believe will make you happy on the list below. Start each with "I would be happy if . . ."

1. _____
_____
_____

2. _____
_____
_____

3. _____
_____
_____

4. _____
_____
_____

5. _____
_____
_____

6. _____
_____
_____

7. _____
_____
_____

8. _____
_____
_____

9. _____
_____
_____

10. _____
_____
_____

of our "happy" wishes are about believing that certain things or situations can make us deep down happy, when that's something only God can do.

There is only one way to get deep down happy that lasts and lasts. It's something God gives and it's called joy. Joy is a deep down happy from God. And joy is what will help you feel happy even when you don't have all you want and even when things aren't going your way.

See, the world's version of "happy" comes and goes. It can fly away if you lose your iPod or if your mom doesn't let you go to a birthday party.

Now look over the list and ask yourself honestly: Are those the things that will keep you happy forever? There's nothing wrong with wishing a certain boy will like you or hoping your parents will break down and get you a cell phone with unlimited texting, but so many

But joy is different. It's a feeling of happy that no one can take away from you. Even if you lose your iPod and your mom is driving you crazy—you can still feel the kind of joy that God gives.

Romans 15:13 says it this way:

> **"May the God of hope fill you with all joy and peace as you trust in him, so that you may overflow with hope by the power of the Holy Spirit." (NIV)**

This verse promises that God fills us with joy when we trust him. Trusting God is the key to having a happy, joyful heart.

It works something like this: Let's say you lose your iPod. You've looked for it everywhere for over a week and it's nowhere to be found. Joy can be found when you stop beating yourself up for losing it, thank God for the time you had it, and realize that you can still enjoy your life without your iPod. While it's a big bummer to lose something you love that much, you can still laugh and play and thank God for your life. That's joy because it's your little way of living out your trust in God. It's your way of remembering that God is in control of everything in your life, whether or not you have an iPod.

When we trust God and believe that he has a good plan for our lives, we experience the deep down God-happy called joy. Does that mean that we will never feel disappointed? No, of course not. We will all have our share of sad times in life—that happens. But we don't have

JOY is your way of remembering that God is in control of EVERYTHING in your life!

to let the sadness take over our life because we can trust God instead.

Jesus even told us that we would have disappointments. In John 16:33 he said:

> **"Here on earth you will have many trials and sorrows. But take heart, because I have overcome the world." (NLT)**

The truth is, there will be unhappy stuff that happens which will bring sadness into our lives, but God has promised to take care of us if we trust him. So my happy wish for you and for me is to hand over our hearts to God and let him fill them up with his kind of happy, the happy that lasts and lasts: Joy! ✳

JUST ❤ BETWEEN ❤ US

1. List three things that make you happy and why they make you happy.

2. What is the difference between happiness and joy?

3. How do you receive joy?

YOU'VE GOT MAIL!!

by Julie Ferwerda

God's Letters Reveal How He Feels about You!

God wants to be your super-close number one BFF!
He's written some pretty awesome things to you in his love letter,
the Bible, so check it out!

When I created you, I made you in my likeness. (see Genesis 5:1)
Wow! to read more, jump to page 15 . . .

the ME-monster

by Susan Jones

When you think of monsters, what's the first thing that pops into your mind? For me, it's Mike Wazowski and Sully from *Monsters, Inc.* That is one of the best movies of all time. Don't you want to snuggle on the couch with Sully? I love laughing out loud at Mike's jokes, crying when Sully says good-bye to "Boo," and sneering at that meanie Randall. Remember him? The one who cheats in the contest to gather the most screams in a single day? He wanted first place so bad that he stole, cheated, and lied to get it. I think he is the perfect representation of a monster. Sneaky, scary (scouwee, as my nephew says), and the big one . . . selfish! Yuck!

the REAL scary thing

Did you know that we all have a little monster living with us? No, she won't show up at night to capture your screams, and she's not hiding in the closet or under your bed. She doesn't always come out, but she's there. Her name? Me-Monster.

I wonder . . . have you met her? She thinks of herself a lot and really hates sharing—especially those brand-new markers with the perfect tips! Sometimes she takes the bigger half of the cookie and gives her little sister the smaller one. And every now and then, she pouts and gives Mom the silent treatment if she doesn't get her way.

Everyone has a little Me-Monster in them. This monster is sneaky, scary, and selfish and can show up when you least expect it. Everything can be rolling along just fine, then out of nowhere, she appears. And when she does, it is NOT a pretty sight. People around her usually don't like to see her because it's a little scary! But the most awful thing about her is a selfish heart. Double Yuck!

the SOURCE of the scary thing

Even Mom and Dad have Me-Monsters. Since Adam and Eve sinned for the very first time in the Garden of Eden, everyone born after them (which is everyone in the world ☺) was born with a "sin nature." That means we were all born with a tendency to think about ourselves all the time, and it takes a lot of effort to think about others and put their needs, wants, and desires above our own. It's kind of a "monster" problem!

the TREATMENT for the scary thing

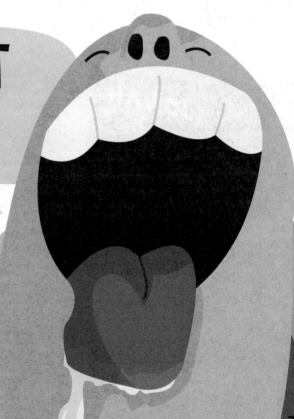

We need help dealing with this problem, and God has given us the treatment in Matthew 22:37–39:

And He said to him, "'YOU SHALL LOVE THE LORD YOUR GOD WITH ALL YOUR HEART, AND WITH ALL YOUR SOUL, AND WITH ALL YOUR MIND.' This is the great and foremost commandment. The second is like it, 'YOU SHALL LOVE YOUR NEIGHBOR AS YOURSELF.'" (NASB)

I'm sure you've heard this verse before, but did you ever notice that before we can love our neighbor as ourselves, we must first love God with all our heart, soul, and mind!?

the GOoD NEWS about the scary thing

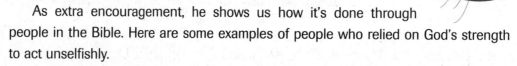

Here's the good news. God knew that being a Me-Monster would be a problem for us, so he gave us his strength and Holy Spirit to help! We certainly couldn't do it alone. So, ask God for his help in making unselfish choices. Once we start doing that regularly, it becomes easier to do!

As extra encouragement, he shows us how it's done through people in the Bible. Here are some examples of people who relied on God's strength to act unselfishly.

- Daniel told King Nebuchadnezzar to keep the gifts that were supposed to be given to him (see Daniel 5:17).
- Abraham gave Lot first pick on his new homeland (see Genesis 13:9).
- Jonah asked to be thrown into the sea because he knew he was causing the storm (see Jonah 1:12–13).

- Joseph stuck by Mary when she was pregnant with Jesus when he didn't have to (see Matthew 1:19–24).
- The apostles (people who spread the news about Jesus after his death) shared their money and houses (see Acts 4:34–35).

   Next time you are tempted to let the Me-Monster surface, remember that God gives us the strength to keep it tucked away. We may not fully ever get rid of it, but we can lock it up and throw away the key. I don't know about you, but the only monsters I want to know are the cute, snuggly ones on the big screen!❋

JUST BETWEEN US

1. What's one example of a time when you've let out the Me-Monster?

2. Why is selfishness so hard to fight?

3. What's your game plan for dealing with selfishness?

ME-monster CRYPTOGRAMS

by Susan Jones

De-code these Bible verses and memorize them to keep that Me-Monster from coming out!

Cryptogram #1

KEY	A	B	C	D	E	F	G	H	I	J	K	L	M	N	O	P	Q	R	S	T	U	V	W	X	Y	Z
	2	16	15	26	7	18	9	24	11	10	6	21	25	4	1	3	12	13	14	17	8	19	5	22	20	23

DON'T BE SELFISH; DON'T
26 1 4 17   16 7   14 7 21 18 11 14 24   26 1 4 17

TRY TO IMPRESS OTHERS. BE
17 13 20   17 1   11 25 3 13 7 14 14   1 17 25 7 13 14   16 7

HUMBLE,
24 8 25 16 21 7   ___ ___ ___ ___ ___ ___ ___ ___ ___ ___ ___ ___ ___ ___ ___
                  17 24 11 4 6 11 4 9   1 18   1 17 24 7 13 14

___ ___   ___ ___ ___ ___ ___ ___   ___ ___ ___ ___ ___ ___ ___ ___ ___ .
2 14   16 7 17 17 7 13   17 24 2 4   20 1 8 13 14 7 21 19 7 14

                                              2:3
___ ___ ___ ___ ___ ___ ___ ___ ___ ___ ___
3 24 11 21 21 11 3 11 2 4 14

Cryptogram #2

KEY	A	B	C	D	E	F	G	H	I	J	K	L	M	N	O	P	Q	R	S	T	U	V	W	X	Y	Z
	2	3	21	14	19	13	22	16	10	17	15	9	25	5	2	7	20	26	23	1	4	11	6	18	12	8

,
___ ___ ___ ___   ___ ___   ___ ___ ___ ___ ___ ___ ___ ___   ___ ___ ___   ___ ___ ___ ___
14 2 5 1   3 19   21 2 5 21 19 26 5 19   13 2 26   12 2 4 26

$$\frac{}{2}\ \frac{}{6}\ \frac{}{5}\quad \frac{}{21}\ \frac{}{2}\ \frac{}{2}\ \frac{}{14}\quad \frac{}{3}\ \frac{}{4}\ \frac{}{1}\quad \frac{}{13}\ \frac{}{2}\ \frac{}{26}$$

$$\frac{}{1}\ \frac{}{16}\ \frac{}{19}\quad \frac{}{22}\ \frac{}{2}\ \frac{}{2}\ \frac{}{14}\quad \frac{}{2}\ \frac{}{13}\quad \frac{}{2}\ \frac{}{1}\ \frac{}{16}\ \frac{}{19}\ \frac{}{26}\ \frac{}{23}\ \textbf{.}$$

1 $\frac{}{21}\ \frac{}{2}\ \frac{}{26}\ \frac{}{10}\ \frac{}{5}\ \frac{}{1}\ \frac{}{16}\ \frac{}{10}\ \frac{}{24}\ \frac{}{5}\ \frac{}{23}$ 10:24

Cryptogram #3
(just a bit harder!)

KEY	A	B	C	D	E	F	G	H	I	J	K	L	M	N	O	P	Q	R	S	T	U	V	W	X	Y	Z
	20			23				11						19						17						

$$\frac{}{5}\ \frac{O}{19}\ \frac{E}{7}\ \frac{I}{23}\quad \frac{}{11}\ \frac{A}{22}\quad \frac{I}{14}\ \frac{E}{20}\ \frac{}{18}\ \frac{}{11}\ \frac{}{23}\ \frac{}{8}\ \frac{}{18}\quad \frac{A}{20}\ \frac{}{8}\ \frac{}{16}\quad \frac{I}{6}\ \frac{}{11}\ \frac{}{8}\ \frac{}{16}\ \textbf{.}$$

$$\frac{}{5}\ \frac{O}{19}\ \frac{E}{7}\ \frac{I}{23}\quad \frac{}{11}\ \frac{}{22}\quad \frac{O}{8}\ \frac{}{19}\ \frac{}{18}\quad \frac{E}{26}\ \frac{A}{23}\ \frac{}{20}\ \frac{O}{5}\ \frac{U}{19}\ \frac{}{17}\ \frac{}{22}\quad \frac{O}{19}\ \frac{}{23}$$

$$\frac{}{1}\ \frac{O}{19}\ \frac{A}{20}\ \frac{}{22}\ \frac{}{18}\ \frac{}{2}\ \frac{U}{17}\ \frac{}{5}\quad \frac{O}{19}\ \frac{}{12}\quad \frac{}{14}\ \frac{O}{12}\ \frac{U}{19}\ \frac{}{17}\ \frac{}{16}\quad \frac{O}{19}\ \frac{}{12}\quad \frac{U}{12}\ \frac{}{17}\ \frac{E}{16}\ \frac{}{23}\ \textbf{.}$$

$$\frac{}{10}\ \frac{A}{20}\ \frac{}{4}\ \textbf{.}\quad \frac{I}{11}\ \frac{}{18}\ \frac{I}{11}\ \frac{}{22}\quad \frac{O}{8}\ \frac{}{19}\ \frac{}{18}\quad \frac{E}{16}\ \frac{A}{23}\ \frac{}{25}\ \frac{}{20}\ \frac{}{8}\ \frac{I}{16}\quad \frac{}{11}\ \frac{}{18}\ \frac{}{22}$$

$$\frac{O}{19}\ \frac{}{10}\ \frac{}{8}\quad \frac{}{10}\ \frac{A}{20}\ \frac{}{4}\ \textbf{.}\quad \frac{I}{11}\ \frac{}{18}\quad \frac{I}{11}\ \frac{}{22}\quad \frac{O}{8}\ \frac{}{19}\ \frac{}{18}\quad \frac{I}{11}\ \frac{}{12}\ \frac{}{12}\ \frac{I}{11}\ \frac{A}{18}\ \frac{}{20}\ \frac{E}{1}\ \frac{}{5}\ \frac{}{23}\ \textbf{,}$$

$$\frac{A}{20}\ \frac{}{8}\ \frac{}{16}\quad \frac{I}{11}\ \frac{}{18}\quad \frac{E}{6}\ \frac{E}{23}\ \frac{}{23}\ \frac{}{14}\ \frac{}{22}\quad \frac{}{8}\ \frac{O}{19}\quad \frac{}{12}\ \frac{E}{23}\ \frac{O}{21}\ \frac{}{19}\ \frac{}{12}\ \frac{}{16}\quad \frac{O}{19}\ \frac{}{2}$$

$$\frac{}{1}\ \frac{E}{23}\ \frac{I}{11}\ \frac{}{8}\ \frac{}{24}\quad \frac{}{10}\ \frac{O}{12}\ \frac{}{19}\ \frac{}{8}\ \frac{E}{24}\ \frac{}{23}\ \frac{}{16}\ \textbf{.}$$

1 $\frac{}{21}\ \frac{O}{19}\ \frac{}{12}\ \frac{I}{11}\ \frac{}{8}\ \frac{}{18}\ \frac{}{15}\ \frac{I}{11}\ \frac{A}{20}\ \frac{}{8}\ \frac{}{22}$ 13:45

SOURCE: www.kidzone.ws/puzzles/cryptogram/crypto.asp

Survey: When I Grow Up I want to Be...

A Veterinarian —*Rachel, 10; Kristin, 12; Lauren, 10; Jessica, 9; Allison, 10; AnnaLee, 10; Keagan, 10*

Singer on American Idol —*Izzy, 8; Zahara. 11; Sarah, 10*

Sunday school teacher —*Grace, 9*

Ranch owner and a mom —*Helen, 12*

A mom —*Valerie, 9; and Anonymous*

Stay at home mom and baker —*Saige, 10*

Missionary or a writer —*Theresa, 12*

Missionary —*Hannah, 11*

Interior designer —*Kaelyn, 12*

Professional horse rider —*Emily, 10; Stephanie, 11; Marissa, 10; Claire, 10*

Horse trainer —*Olivia, 9*

Photographer —*Tate, 10; Gabi, 12*

A cook/chef
—Ashley, 9

Something to do with animals that does not include blood but does include babies. —Casie, 10

Actress
—Jessica, 8; Ellie, 9; Breanna, 12; Ashton, 10; Mileah, 12

Actress and author/illustrator
—Stephanie, 10½

Singer
—Anne, 11; Faith, 9; Savannah, 12; Kelly, 12; Mikaela, 10; Elise, 10

An attorney/lawyer
—Laura, 10; Corrie, 11; Joclyn, 11; Corinne, 11

Professional gymnast —Kaleigh, 10

Teacher
—Kayla, 10; Danielle, 11; Alex, 10; Gia, 9; Elizabeth, 10; Laney, 9; Samantha, 10; Hope, 8; Allison, 8½; Angela, 8; Caroline, 9

Preschool teacher —Lauren, 11; Victoria, 8

Dog trainer
—Kristie, 11

Author
—Chloe, 9; Amber, 9; Elisa, 11

Professional cheerleader
—Taylor, 11

Actress and accountant
—Gretchen, 11¾

Actress (on Broadway)
—Danielle, 11

Actress/singer
—Andie, 12½

Hairstylist —Jaimee, 10

Nurse
—Alex, 11

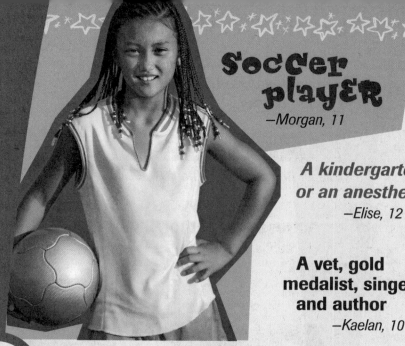

Soccer player
—Morgan, 11

A kindergarten teacher or an anesthesiologist
—Elise, 12

A vet, gold medalist, singer, and author
—Kaelan, 10

Fashion designer
—Melissa, 9; Grace, 8;
Lara, 11½; Breanna, 11

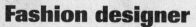

Own an orphanage
—Melissa, 11

Doctor
—Molly, 11; Anonymous

Psychiatrist
—Amy, 12

Zoologist
—Mara, 10; Kennan, 8

Ballerina & a good Christian woman —Katie, 9 ½

Pet sitter
—Merissa, 10

A singer, designer, or a writer
—Emma, 9½

Children's dentist
—Brooke, 11

An Olympic swimmer
—Riley, 10

Marine biologist
—Brittani, 11

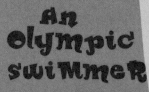

Worship leader *—Kelsey, 12*

The first woman president of the United States
—Mayson, 11

Artist
—Bethany, 12

Architect & missionary
—Brittany, 10

YOU'VE GOT MAIL!!

God's Letters Reveal How He Feels about You!

When you cry out to me, I will pay attention, for I'm compassionate. (see Exodus 22:27)

Out of everyone on earth, I've chosen you to be my treasured daughter. (see Deuteronomy 14:2)

I'll never leave you or abandon you. (see Deuteronomy 31:8)

Not one of my good promises has ever failed to come true. (see Joshua 23:14)

I'll strengthen you when your heart is fully committed to me. (see 2 Chronicles 16:9)

I gave you life, showed you kindness, and watched over your spirit. (see Job 10:12)

Can you believe it?! Want more? turn to page 25 . . .

Quiz

R U A Cliquey-chick?

by Julie Ferwerda

Find out if being one of the crowd is your thing.

1. Being a friend means:

A) Showing kindness to others, regardless of who they are.

B) Being there for people you already know and like.

C) Hanging with popular people who improve your reputation.

2. If your buds were trashing a nice girl outside your group you would:

A) Stick up for her.

B) Change the subject or keep quiet.

C) Add your two cents so they know you're in.

3. Your group is headed to a movie this weekend you don't care to see, so you:

A) Make other plans and invite someone outside your group.
B) Stall until you figure out how to get out of it.
C) Tag along because you don't want to be left out.

4. A new girl in your class doesn't have anyone to eat lunch with, so you:

A) Invite her to join you and your friends.
B) Ask your friends if they want to sit with her.
C) Let her find someone else to eat with.

5. When it comes to the latest fashions, your friends:

A) All have their own style.
B) Consult each other before big events.
C) Dress like each other.

6. Your coolest friend is sleeping over and your sis asks you to play a little kid game with her. You:

A) Ask your friend if you both can play one game with her.
B) Tell sis you'll play with her after your friend leaves.
C) Tell sis to get lost.

7. Your friends ask you to lie to your parents so you can watch a PG-13 movie. You:

A) Tell your parents the truth and start looking for some new kids to hang out with.
B) Tell your friends you'll sit this one out.
C) Make it happen.

Total up your answers. How many A's, B's, and C's did you have?

Mostly A: One Radical Chick—You're not afraid to go against the flow to be a good friend to others (even if they're different than you), and to make right choices. If necessary, you'll most likely find new friends before being influenced to become someone you don't want to be. While standing up for what's right and being an individual, try not to be "in your face" about it, or you'll get a bad rap for being a snob, and that could hurt your chances of having a good influence on others.

Mostly B: Not 2 Clique-y—While you aren't too easily influenced, you haven't made up your mind completely about following the crowd. You want the best of both worlds—pleasing your friends and keeping your values—which is a losing game. Remember it's super easy to be pulled down and hard to get back up. Make up your mind ahead of the game as to what you won't do with the crowd, find your own groove, and stick to it.

Mostly C: Vanilla Groupie—If you were ice cream, you'd be vanilla, cuz you're not living out your own unique God-given flavor. Following the in-crowd too closely will give you the wrong reputation and will eventually lead to trouble. "Do not be misled: 'Bad company corrupts good character'" (1 Corinthians 15:33 NIV). It's time to play by some new rules—welcome some new pals into your life and get your own identity before you have regrets. ✳

If I Could Change One Thing...

by Vicki Courtney

We surveyed girls your age and asked them what one thing they would change about themselves, if it were possible. Interestingly, most girls said they would change "nothing," which is awesome! That means that many girls your age are comfortable with the person God created them to be. Of course, that doesn't mean that we don't struggle from time to time with wishing we could change something about ourselves whether it's appearance related or more about character qualities.

One thing I noticed about the survey answers was that most of the girls who wanted to change something, mentioned something related to their appearance. A few girls mentioned things related to their character or behavior. That tells me that many girls are feeling pressure to look a certain way and it's important that you know that each and every one of you is beautiful just as you are. You are created in God's image! In fact, did you know that *girls in the 1800s and early 1900s were more concerned with their character and behavior (being patient, loving, kind, etc.) rather than their appearance?* Many of these girls didn't even have mirrors in their homes and they certainly didn't have TV shows, magazines, and movies with perfect looking girls in them! If you ask me, I think we could learn a thing or two from these women of the past. **There's nothing wrong with wanting to change something about our character or behavior, especially as we are trying to be more like God. What about you? Are you more focused with changing something on the outside or the inside?**

Survey: If you could change one thing about yourself, what would it be?

Nothing; I like myself the way I am; I like how God made me.
—Zahara, 11; Gia, 9; Claire, 10; Elizabeth, 10; Sydney, 10; Molly, 11; Mara, 10; April, 11; Madeleine, 10; Elise, 10; Lauren, 10; Stephanie, 11; Emily, 10; Laura, 10; Jordyn, 9; Lisa, 8½; Kimberley, 11; Meagan, 10; Morgan, 11; Caroline, 9; Kelsey, 12; Taylor, 11; Angela, 12; Riley, 11; Joclyn, 11

Nothing. I like myself the way I am.
—Addison, 11

To be skinnier —Anne, 11

Taller —Grace, 9

I'd be better at math —Theresa, 12

I would have no braces
—Savannah, 12

My habit of biting my nails
—Kayla, 10

I would be outgoing —Danielle, 11

Being able to speak up about my feelings —Kristie, 11

Change my hair color to reddish-orange because my best friend has that color
—Kristin, 12

That I could control my anger better
—Emily, 10

My hair —Alex, 10; Karly, 9; Rachel, 10; Mikaela, 10; Merissa, 10

Hair color
—Allison, 10; Samantha, 10; Allison, 8½

My hair because I want it to be straight and more blonde
—Kennan, 8

My hair, I want it to be blonde
—Corinne, 11

My body —Chloe, 9

How I act at school —Taylor, 11

My attitude —Casie, 10

My teeth —Valerie, 9; Kaleigh, 10; Marissa, 10; Gretchen, 11

That I didn't have allergies
—Jessica, 8

Height —Julie, 11

Not to be allergic to food
—Jaimee, 10

Be older —Olivia, 9

That I didn't have dry skin
—Bethany, 12

I would be more trustworthy
—Kaelan, 10

No freckles —Ellie, 9

I would change my temper
—Jessica, 9

That I would learn to dance
—Breanna, 12

That I worship God more
—Morgan, 10

My personality —AnnaLee, 10

My tummy, it kinda sticks out
—Melissa, 9

No glasses —Laney, 9

I would like not to be dyslexic so school
would be easier
—Melissa, 11

My glasses. They itch me
—Stephanie, 10½

Not have to have glasses
—Hope, 8

Be a better friend —Grace, 8

I would change my temper
—Mileah, 12

My legs —Lara, 11½; Andie, 12½

Be a faster runner —Amy, 12

To be left-handed instead of right-handed —Morgan, 11

I wish I didn't have warts
—Emily, 12

The way my voice sounds (I have a deep
voice and I don't like it) —Brooke, 11

To have perfect vision —Saige, 10

My vision —Anne, 8

My weight —Angela, 8

Freckles/face —Brittani, 11

My height —Nicole, 9

My attitude —Amber, 9

My eye color —Faith, 11

The size of my feet —Jenica, 11

My tendency to fear about the future instead of think about the great things God is doing now —Mayson, 11

To sin less —Anonymous, 11

My voice. I have a really low voice and I wish it would be a little higher —Karon, 11

To make my zits go away forever —Emma, 9

That I wouldn't be so hard on myself. I know it's good to push yourself, but not to be tough on yourself when you fall a little short of your expectations —Courtney, 11

I would want to be taller because I am small. People call me shrimp! —Breeann, 11

That I could run faster —Rachel, 11

My name —Danielle, 9

I would be more loving to my sisters —Alyssa, 8

My ears —Julia, 11

I would not need glasses. But I know that God made me just right —Ellie, 11

I wish I was more outgoing —Sarah Grace, 10

I would have perfect feet instead of a crooked toe, bunion, and walking on the inside of my feet, which is the way they are now. —Sami, 11

I would be REALLY popular at school —Heather, 9½ ✳

QUIZ

WHO'S RUNNING the Show?

by Vicki Courtney

volleyball dance

1. You are good at both dance and volley-ball, but your parents won't let you do both because it will take up too much of your time in the school year. They tell you to choose one sport, but you don't want to make a decision you will regret. You . . .

A) take out a sheet of paper and make two columns. You list the pros and cons of volleyball and dance. Dance wins—I mean, if you stick with it, you can be on the drill team someday and that's what the popular girls do, right?

B) ask your three closest friends what you should pick and go with the majority. Besides, you don't want to pick one sport and then find out they chose the other one!

C) take it before God and ask him to make it very clear to you. God reminds you that some of the dance moves the older girls do in their performances are not appropriate. If you stick it out in dance, you might be faced with some tough decisions down the road. Not as many of your friends do volleyball, but the truth is, you enjoy it more than dance.

2. There's a new girl at your church who will be in your same grade at school. Your mom encourages you to invite her over to meet some of your friends. You . . .

A) grumble and complain because it will be so awkward. What in the world will you talk about? What will your friends think?

B) tell your mom OK, but call your friends and warn them in advance that it wasn't your idea. If they don't like the new girl, you won't either.

C) tell your mom it's a great idea and ask if it would be OK to have her spend the night too. You can't imagine how it would feel to be in a new town and starting a new school and not know anyone. Besides, it's the right thing to do . . . it's what God would want you to do.

3. Some of your friends are allowed to IM and want you to get a screen name so you can all IM together. You . . .

A) set the account up without telling your parents.

B) let your friends set up the account for you. That way, if mom and dad find out, you can blame your friends.

C) tell your friends you'll have to talk to your parents first and get their approval. Even if they say no, asking them is the right thing to do.

4. One of your friends asks if you are going to an upcoming sleepover that another one of your friends is having over the weekend. At least you thought she was your friend—you weren't invited! You . . .

A) cry yourself to sleep that night. This girl has been tacky to you before, but there has to be a way to get invited to that party. You dig in your closet the next morning for your new shirt she recently complimented. If you give it to her, maybe she'll invite you.

B) ask your mom to call the girl's mom and find out why you weren't invited. Who knows, maybe she can work her magic and get you an invitation to the party!

C) shed a few tears when you go to bed that night and pray about it. You talk to God about how sad you are feeling and ask him to help you deal with the disappoint-ment. God's in control even if it doesn't make much sense right now. Who knows, maybe he's trying to protect you from spending too much time with this girl!

5. You try out for a lead part in the upcoming school play. You have practiced the lines for weeks and everyone thinks you'll get the part. The only problem is that the drama teacher's daughter is also trying out for the part. Sure enough, she gets it, even though she flubbed up her lines during the audition. You . . .

A) approach your drama teacher and tell her it's not fair. You are so much better than her daughter and everyone seems to know it.
B) call good ol' Mom. She can fix the problem!
C) pray about it and decide to trust God with the details even if they aren't always fair. You ask him to help you have a good attitude about the part you have been given and give it your best.

Total up your answers. How many A's, B's, and C's did you have?

Self-paced program (Mostly A): You are in charge of your destiny. When you take God out of the picture and run the show, you miss God's plan and purpose for your life. Doing what you want to do seems to be more important than doing what God wants you to do. You need to do a serious heart check and start leaning on God more (reading your Bible and praying) when making choices in life.

Friends and family plan (Mostly B): You rely on others more than God when making choices in life. Whether you're giving into peer pressure or counting on Mom to solve your problems, you've still taken the matter out of God's hands. Your friends and family can't possibly know you or the situation like God does. Sometimes God doesn't give us the answer we want to hear, but in the end God wants us to trust him with the details.

Father knows best (Mostly C): When it comes to making choices, it looks like you are in the habit of letting God run the show. Good for you! When you are older and making important decisions about your career path, who you will marry, and other life choices, you will be less likely to stray from his plan and purpose for your life.

Proverbs 3:5-6 says,

"Trust GOD from the bottom of your heart;
   don't try to figure out everything on your own.
   Listen for GOD's voice in everything you do, everywhere you go;
   he's the one who will keep you on track. *(The Message)* ✳

YOU'VE GOT MAIL!!

God's Letters Reveal How He Feels about You!

You are glorious—all my delight is in you. (see Psalm 16:3)

I rescued you because I delighted in you. (see Psalm 18:19)

Even if your father and mother abandon you,
I'll always love and keep you. (see Psalm 27:10)

I will counsel you and watch over you. (see Psalm 32:8)

I'll deliver you from all your fears. (see Psalm 34:4)

I'm close to you when you're brokenhearted. (see Psalm 34:18)

Delight yourself in me, and I will give you your heart's desires. (see Psalm 37:4)

I'm captivated by your beauty. (see Psalm 45:11)

I'll be your guide to the very end. (see Psalm 48:14)

I don't withhold anything good from you when you obey me. (see Psalm 84:11–12)

My love for you is higher than the heavens;
my faithfulness reaches to the skies. (see Psalm 108:4)

My word helps you find your way, like a bright light on a dark path. (see Psalm 119:105)

I discipline you because I love you. (see Proverbs 3:12)

My name is a strong tower. Call to me always and be safe. (see Proverbs 18:10)

Though your sins are red as scarlet, I will make them white as snow. (see Isaiah 1:18)

If you trust in me, I will give you perfect peace. (see Isaiah 26:3)

I long to be gracious to you; I rise up to show you compassion. (see Isaiah 30:18)

I gather you in my arms and carry you close to my heart. (see Isaiah 40:11)

When you hope in me, I will renew your strength. (see Isaiah 40:31)

Still not convinced? Turn to page 31 for more . . .

Body Development:
what's your one worry?

by Vicki Courtney

When we surveyed girls your age, we asked them if they had any worries about body development. Most girls were worried about starting their period, which, by the way, is completely normal! In fact, we included an article on page 28 that should hopefully be a big help to the girls who may have some questions or worries about getting their period. We also have an article about—are you ready for this?—boobs. There, I said it. Boobs, boobs, boobs. Don't blush! It's part of being a woman! You can find that article on page 32.

In fact, all the answers we got are completely normal things that many girls worry about. The important thing to remember is that God has "fearfully and wonderfully" made you (Psalm 139:14) Take peace in knowing that you will develop at the pace he has determined and have the exact body shape that he intended. Body shape is different than weight. That doesn't mean that God's OK with you eating everything in sight and being overweight.

He wants you to be healthy and eat right, especially during this important time in your life when your body is developing. That means being in a healthy weight range—not too thin and not too heavy. In the meantime, no worries! He has everything under control!

Survey: *When it comes to body development, what is one thing you're kinda-sorta worried about?*

- Starting my period *(see Periods: End of a Sentence or Beginning of Womanhood? on page 28)* —*Savannah, 12; Kayla, 10; Danielle, 11; Kelly, 12; Alex, 10; Karly, 9; Chloe, 9; Jaimee, 10; Jessica, 9; Elise, 10; Allison, 10; Riley, 10*

- ***My period might start at school*** —*Corrie, 11*

- That when my chest develops, it will draw attention —*Taylor, 11*

- Getting fat —*Casie, 10; Emily, 10*

- **Being the last one to develop** —*Elise, 12*

- Boys staring at me when I start developing —*Rachel, 10*

- ***Not being physically strong. I'm really skinny and I'm not curvy!*** —*Bethany, 12*

- Not being tall or having big enough boobs —*Kaelan, 10*

- That I won't develop in certain places —*Breanna, 12*

- ***Not being tall enough*** —*Sarah, 10*

- Getting fat, I always want to stay fit—it really worries me. —*Keagan, 10*

- That I'll be too tall and clumsy —*Morgan, 11*

- **That people will look at me different because I'm maturing faster than my friends** —*Emily, 12* ✳

#%$periods...

End of a Sentence or the Beginning of Womanhood

by Susie Davis

You have probably heard girls your age talking about periods. And I don't mean the period that comes at the end of a sentence—you know, like an exclamation mark or a question mark. I'm talking about the period that girls talk about when they say things like, "I'm on my period." Or maybe, "I hope I don't get my period this weekend because I'm supposed to go to Amy's swim party." You know . . . that period.

You might have heard girls talk about stuff like that and been curious as well as a little confused. You probably know that you'll get a period someday (if you haven't already), but you have a lot of questions about what a period is and how it happens in your body. Let me reassure you, your questions are normal. Very normal. And the best place to get the information you're looking for is from your mother or your doctor. I know it

might seem embarrassing to ask them, but that's where you will find the best answers to your questions. Though it's probably easier just to listen to your friends talk about their periods and try to figure it out yourself, the truth is sometimes there's some pretty weird information floating around out there. And some of it is just wrong. So it's really best to get the info from an expert. Yep, that's your mom or your doctor. Just remember that you're not silly for asking questions about how your body works and you're not the first to feel a little embarrassed about your "private parts."

Just to get you started, how about this? I will try and answer the top ten questions from girls your age. But remember, if anything seems especially confusing, be sure and ask your mom.

Question One: *Why is it called a period?*

The name doctor's use for a period is menstrual cycle, menses, or menstrual period. None of those are super easy to say so women everywhere have come up with lots of different nicknames for the menstrual cycle and "period" happens to be the most popular one.

Question Two: *What all happens during a period?*

What a woman's body does during a period is really amazing but the info can be pretty complicated to explain. So at your age, I would say ask your mom about it. She's going to be the best one to tell you about how the whole thing works. Maybe the two of you could go to the library and check out some books about body development. There are tons of wonderful books that will explain the whole thing in detail.

Question Three: *When will I start my period?*

This one is hard to answer because I don't know anything about how your body is growing; plus, I'm not a doctor. I can tell you that most girls start their periods anywhere between the ages of eight and seventeen. And the girls who start on the very early or very late side should probably talk with their doctor or get a check-up to make sure all is well.

Question Four: *I started my period but my friends haven't. Am I normal?*

It's normal to wonder if your body is working like it's supposed to—especially if you are comparing yourself to the girls around you. On one hand, it's hard to have already started your period when your friends haven't, especially if you are still in grade school. And on the other hand, maybe your friends who haven't started worry about whether they will ever get a period at all. It's really important to remember that every body grows at different speeds. And it's best not to worry about how fast or slow your body is growing; instead, talk to your mom about your questions, and if you need to, visit with your doctor.

Question Five: *Does it hurt to have a period?*

No, it doesn't hurt to have your period. Sometimes women have cramps in their tummy area when they are having their period and they can feel uncomfortable, but cramps are fixable. Most women solve their period cramps by taking Advil or Tylenol, just like you would for a headache.

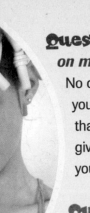

Question Six: *I'm worried people will know when I'm on my period. Will they?*

No one can tell when you are on your period. But when you start your period, it's a good idea to keep track of it on a calendar so that you'll know when to expect it. There are tips your mom can give you to make sure you are well-prepared when you start your period.

Question Seven: *I'm scared I will start my period for the first time at school. What do I do if that happens?*

It's a worry for many girls. If you do happen to start your period at school, go to the school nurse. She will give you what you need and will likely even let you call your mom.

Question Eight: *My friends told me that periods make girls fat. Will my period make me fat?*

Absolutely not. Your period will not make you fat. But you will get curvier. Your hips and breasts will get rounder. But these changes don't mean that you are "getting fatter." They actually mean that you are becoming more womanly, which is exactly what your body is designed to do.

Question Nine: *The whole idea of getting a period really grosses me out. Will I always feel this way?*

It's doubtful. When you do start your period, you will be older and better able to handle all the changes your body is going through. It might seem easier to stay a little girl forever but that's not really true. When your body starts to change, your ideas about things will change and you might actually look forward to having a more grown-up body. Give yourself time and for now, enjoy being right where you are—a girl who is fearfully and wonderfully made by God inside and out. ✱

YOU'VE GOT MAIL!!

God's Letters Reveal How He Feels about You!

Do not fear . . . I am with you.
I am your God and I will help you. (see Isaiah 41:10)

You are mine. (see Isaiah 43:2)

I have swept away your sins like the morning mist. (see Isaiah 44:22)

Apart from me there is no God who can
help you or save you. (see Isaiah 45:6)

Even when you are old with gray hair,
I will sustain you and carry you. (see Isaiah 46:4)

My unfailing love for you will never be shaken. (see Isaiah 54:10)

When you cry for help, I will say, "Here I am." (see Isaiah 58:9)

I will always guide you and satisfy your needs. (see Isaiah 58:11)

As a bridegroom rejoices over his bride, so I will rejoice over you. (see Isaiah 62:5)

Before I formed you in your mother's womb,
I knew you and set you apart. (see Jeremiah 1:5)

I have plans to help you succeed, and to give you hope and a future. (see Jeremiah 29:11)

I love you with everlasting love; I've drawn you close
with loving-kindness. (see Jeremiah 31:3)

I will turn your sadness into happiness. (see Jeremiah 31:13)

I will refresh you when you are worn out. (see Jeremiah 31:25)

I take great delight in you, soothing you with my love
and singing over you. (see Zephaniah 3:17)

I'm with you always, to the very end of the world. (see Matthew 28:20)

Nothing is impossible with me. (see Luke 1:37)

I came to give you life to the max. (John 10:10)

Gotta hear more? Turn to page 47 . . .

don't be a boob

by Susie Davis

Boobs—that's kind of a weird word and doctors actually call them breasts but who in the world goes around calling them that? If you look up boob in the dictionary it says: a stupid, awkward person. That's actually kind of how I remember feeling when I was just starting to get boobs— like a stupid, awkward girl. So to keep you from feeling stupid at this time of your life, I'm going to answer some of the top questions girls your age have about breasts. Because the truth is that it is good for you to understand your body, even the parts that make you feel a little embarrassed. You should know what your body does, how it works and what all the parts are called. By learning a little more info about what's growing there right under your chin, you will feel more confident and less like a stupid, awkward person. Hopefully, you won't feel like a "boob" yourself!

1.

Question One: Why do girls even have boobs in the first place? Well, one reason is your breasts are developing to feed your future children. You know—breastfeeding. Oh, I know, I know. That's a million years away. Of course it is, but when you grow up, and if you have children someday a million years from now—your breasts will be able to make milk for a baby. As a matter of fact, doctors say that breast milk is the perfect food for an infant. And that's pretty amazing. Aside from that, your breasts grow larger to give you a curvy, womanly figure.

2.

Question Two: I heard someone talking about breast buds. What are breast buds and when will I get them? Breast buds are a small knot that grows right under your nipple. Sometimes you can't even see it but you can usually feel it. At times, it might be a little tender but that tenderness usually goes away. (If not, be sure to ask your mom about it.) Girls usually get breast buds between the ages of seven and thirteen. They are the beginning sign that your breasts are starting to grow. It's as if your breast is budding, much like a flower starts to bud before it blooms. If you can feel a small knot under your nipple or if you notice a slight pucker at your nipple, you likely have breast buds. Sometimes, one nipple develops a breast bud before the other and that's quite normal. No worries. The one will catch up with the other and even out.

3.

Question Three: What if my boobs are too small or too big? Too small or big? For what? Your breasts will develop according to the way God designed your body—just right. Don't get tricked into worrying about whether or not your body will look "perfect" because "perfect" changes all the time. Way back when in the 1950s—big boobs were in. They were "perfect." Then, ten years later in the 1960s—little boobs were in. They were "perfect." Learn this important truth right now: As the years go by, the standard for what the world thinks is beautiful and perfect will change. Back and forth the styles will swing. The best thing you can do (especially since you really have no control over how big or small your breasts will become) is to thank God for how wonderfully your body is made. Thank him that he designed you so carefully and thoughtfully . . . big boobs or small.

4.

Question Four: Will I get hair under my arms when I get boobs? Yes, it is highly likely you will grow hair under your arms when your breasts start to develop. It's quite normal. And it's also quite normal to want to shave that hair right off so that you don't end up looking like a man! If you start to get underarm hair, ask your mom for a razor. It's the same kind of razor that you will likely want to use on your legs if you aren't already.

5.

Question Five: When should I wear a bra? That's really a great question for you to talk over with your mom. But my thinking is that when you start to feel embarrassed about not wearing one—that is the time to start wearing one. It's also good to wear a bra if you are doing a lot of sports because sports bras, in particular, are perfect for protecting the soft tissue that starts developing when your breasts get larger. You don't want to be running all over the place on the soccer field or at a dance class without protection.

So there, just a smidge of information about not being a stupid, awkward girl that doesn't know anything at all about her own body. Don't be a boob! Stay informed! ✳

10 SUPER COOL THINGS about: YOU

by Julie Ferwerda

1. You have 60,000 miles of blood vessels cruising through your body (more than twice the distance around the earth)

2. Your heart beats over 100,000 times a day

3. You have 639 muscles with at least 6,000,000,000 muscle fibers each

4. While reading this sentence, 50,000 cells in your body will die and be replaced

5. You produce 4 cups of saliva every day

6. A sneeze zooms out of your mouth at over 100 m.p.h.

7. You spent about 1 to 2 hours as a single cell

8. Your brain generates more electrical impulses in a day than all the telephones in the world put together

9. Your eye can distinguish 500 shades of gray

10. You have approximately 100,000 hairs on your head

Quiz

Can you keep a secret?

by Julie Ferwerda

"A gossip betrays a confidence, but a trustworthy person keeps a secret." *(Proverbs 11:13 NIV)*
Follow the flow chart below to see where you stack up on the trust scale!

Start

never tell a soul, not even your diary.

Your mom needs your advice on what kind of gaming system to get your brother for Christmas—a whole month away. He's been dying for a gaming system! You . . .

After swearing you to secrecy, your BFF (best friend forever) tells you she's stressed cuz her parents aren't getting along too well lately. You . . .

have to tell someone, so you tell your sister after she tells you a big secret first.

Big sis tells you she's planning a huge surprise party for mom and dad's anniversary. You . . .

SecRets SaFe:

Spilling the beans is not your style. You'd rather let a secret hide in the dark than take credit or get anyone in trouble (or hurt their reputation). Your skilled secret-keeping makes you a totally trustworthy friend. Be careful though—there are some secrets that need to be told, like if someone's in danger. When in doubt, run it by your parents.

ModeRately MuZzLed:

You try hard to keep secrets, but sometimes temptation to tell gets the best of you. Better to keep the details in silence by changing the subject, not dwelling on the latest info, or letting friends know you just don't want to know everything. Also, remember how it feels to have your secrets revealed, and use that feeling to work on becoming more tight-lipped.

LOoSe Lips:

Everyone knows they can come to you for juicy info, but not to trust you with theirs unless they want to see it on the billboard. Realize that when you tell all, you're not improving your image, you're hurting it and the person you're telling on. It's not too late to earn a new reputation, but you've got a lot of work to do. It's time to zip it up and become a trustworthy person.

feel terrible for everyone on the list while waiting for the coach to post it.

let everyone who's not on the list know—you're just trying to help.

You're the first to find out who got cut from the team when you accidentally see a private paper on your coach's desk. You . . .

decide it's none of your business and forget about it.

suck it up because you'd rather let him be totally surprised.

You overhear your teacher tell the principal that one of your classmates flunked the whole semester. You . . .

tell all your friends at lunch.

tell her you'd rather not say cuz it's a private matter.

let on that you know what he's getting and totally rub it in.

keep your lips sealed and help her get everything ready.

finally get a clue and clam up.

The most popular girl in school wants in on the juicy flunk-gossip and asks what you overheard. You . . .

happily fill her in on the details. Maybe now she'll want to hang out sometime.

drop hints like crazy all week, acting like you know something they don't.

"Somehow," mom and dad figure out the scoop, but they ask you to keep it to yourself that they know. You . . .

let your brother know they know and it gets back to your sis. Oops.

by Vicki Courtney

Are you CELL-Mannered?

OK, so you finally got that new cell phone you've been begging your parents for and you can't wait to yak it up with your friends. Here are 10 rules to help you become a cell-mannered girl:

1) Turn off your phone in places where you know they're not allowed. Even if they're allowed, resist the urge to answer if you are in a place where others might consider it rude! (church, weddings, school assemblies, plays, concerts, movie theaters, etc.)

2) Never talk while you are in a bathroom. It doesn't matter if it's your bathroom at home or a public bathroom—don't do it! No one wants to hear a toilet flushing in the background while they're talking to you nor do others in the bathroom want to hear you talking while they are going to the bathroom. Rude, rude, rude!

3) Never talk or text when you are having a conversation with others. If you think the call is important (like, your mom), say, "Excuse me for a minute. I need to get this." Step away and take the call and then apologize when you return. No one likes to be interrupted, so unless it's an important call, chances are it can wait..

4) Never talk or text on your phone while having a meal. It doesn't matter if you're at home in your kitchen or at a restaurant. The only exception is if you are expecting a call from Mom or Dad or a similar emergency. In that case, excuse yourself from the table to take the call.

5} Never send pictures or texts from someone else's phone and pretend to be them. You should never use someone's phone without their permission.

6} Do not call or text your friends at inappropriate hours. Chances are, their parents will eventually find out and it could give them a bad impression of you.

7} If your phone has a camera or video feature, never take inappropriate pictures and send them to others. Never take pictures of strangers or anyone for that matter, without their permission.

8} Never talk loud on your phone while in enclosed spaces with other people (airplanes, cars, elevators, waiting rooms, etc.). If possible, wait until you are in a larger space to talk. If you must take or make a call, talk very quiet and keep it brief!

9} Be sensitive to those around you while using your phone. Sometimes it's easy to be off in your own little world while talking to someone and forget others are nearby. Don't scream, laugh loudly, or behave in such a manner as to draw attention to yourself.

10} Follow the rules your parents have given you. Maybe you only have a cell phone for emergency purposes. You are not alone. That's how most kids start out. It is your job to prove to your parents that you can be trusted with a cell phone. If you follow their rules, you have a better chance of them adding other privileges on down the road (more minutes, text messaging, etc.). ✳

me, myself, and I ✳ between us girls   39 ✳ ✳ ✳ ✳

Words of Wisdom
from Teen Girls
Who Have

been there

done that

We've all needed advice before, and it's especially nice if it comes from someone who has been in our shoes before. When we surveyed girls your age, we asked what questions you have about going into middle school. We thought it would be a great idea to turn your questions over to some high school girls who were happy to pass along their advice.

The best way to deal with these girls is to kill them with kindness. I know it sounds cheesy, but when they look back, they will remember how nice you were to them. Maybe your actions will make them want to be different. —Cayla, 14

Just be confident in who you are, because if you can be confident and comfortable with who you are, the "mean girls" comments and looks can't hurt you. —Sarah, 14

For the most part, just try to ignore them. Chances are, if they see that their comments aren't affecting you, they'll stop. Also, try talking to a parent, a counselor, or someone you trust. —Kaitlyn, 15

Try not to let what others say bother you. A lot of girls say mean things just to try to make themselves look better. Just be nice to those people who are mean to you and don't act like it bothers you and it won't be as fun for them. Oh, and one more thing—pray about it! God definitely cares about what upsets his daughters! —Stephanie, 18

Prayer and love! So many times girls are mean because of things that go on in their home or for different reasons they are hurting on the inside. Love them through Christ! In 1 John 3:18 (look it up!) Jesus tells us to SHOW our love, not just merely say it! Show the love of Christ to everyone, even the mean girls! —Jennifer, 15

Mean girls are insecure with themselves and are willing to put down any other person to build themselves up. It is best just to ignore them and build up a true group of friends around you whom you know WILL stick up for you when these insecure girls are really brutal. —Alicia, 17

I have dealt with my fair share of "mean girls," and I find the best way of "dealing" with them is to not let it affect you! They are probably saying and doing these things to you because they have a problem in their own lives! Always remember, the number one way of dealing with them is through prayer! God holds everything in his hands and he will be there for you no matter what! —Emily, 16

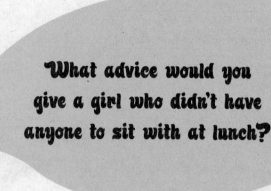

This is a wonderful opportunity to meet someone new and make a good friend. There have been times when I didn't know anyone at lunch, but I wouldn't have met some of the good friends I have now if I had stuck to my usual friends, and not talked to someone new. —Katie, 13

God says to ask and you will receive. Don't be afraid to ask him for godly girlfriends who will stick by you until the end, even at lunch. —Cayla, 14

You had friends in grade school, so sit with the old familiar faces. And for the new girls, just make new friends: sit down, and be like "Hey I'm _____!" and maybe if the girl is wearing a cute shirt, be like "I love your shirt, I saw it at _____." —Sarah, 14

Don't be afraid to go and sit with a group of people you don't know. Be open to talking, and you'll probably make some new friends! Also, introduce yourself to people in your classes throughout the morning. Then, by the time you get to lunch, you'll know some people. —Katilyn, 15

Instead of waiting for someone to come to you, find someone else who looks like they could use a friend. Reach out to them! Think of others and put them before yourself. Who knows, you might find that person sitting by herself will be your new best friend. —Stephanie, 18

If you already have a friend at the school, ask her to introduce you to more of her friends and hang with them for lunch, or find someone with the same fear you do, or who looks overwhelmed and scared . . . talk to her, who knows, this could be your best friend some day. Do what you would give a million dollars to somebody to do to you at that moment. —Maria, 14

For the first half of my freshman year of high school, I had no real "Lunch Table." I would sit anywhere. Lots of people would sit at my table but they never talked to me. It wasn't their fault, I just never made eye contact with them. So why would they think I was interested in talking with them? After a while I made friends with people who were into theatre and did plays with me and I began to search for them at lunch. One day I finally spotted them at a table all the way across the lunch room from my normal spot. I came to the table and asked if I could sit with them and they thought I was silly for not finding them earlier. Guess what, I'm still friends with all of them and I'm still sitting with most of them! —Alicia, 17

If you play on a sports team, try to sit next to a girl on your team. If not, then sit with a girl who sits next to you in class and seems friendly. —Alli, 14

Instead of thinking about how you don't have anyone to sit with, think about the other girls who don't have anyone to sit with. If you see a girl all alone with her head down, go talk to her. Look at others' needs instead of your own. This is how I met my best friend in middle school and we're still very close. —Morgan, 15

How did/do you deal with cliques in school?

Everywhere you go, cliques will be. Don't try to act like something you're not just to fit in with a clique. God will supply you with great friends if you just ask him to. —Cayla, 14

Cliques, oh goodness. The thing about cliques is just that everyone is so insecure and they can't handle not being the center of attention. Just find a good group of friends and stick with them; that way you're too busy having fun with your friends instead of dealing with the insecure girls that are in the cliques. —Sarah, 14

Cliques will follow you wherever you go, even after middle school. Sadly, it's just a part of life. Just be yourself. True friends will love you for who you are and will stick with you through thick and thin.—Kaitlyn, 15

Don't worry about having to be in the popular crowd. A lot of times those who are popular or in cliques are the least happy! Find a good, true friend who will stick by you through everything! —Stephanie, 18

Every school has cliques! There is almost no way around them! But that does not mean that you have to be a part of one, or feel left out because you are not in one! Just find a nice group of friends who like you for you, and not because you meet their criteria! But remember, if you are in a "group" of girls that you do not think is a clique, stand back for a second, examine it, and ask yourself, "How do we treat others?" and "Are we accepting of others?" If you answer "Not good" and "No," then maybe it is time to re-adjust your situation! —Emily, 16

> ## How did you handle having to switch class and learn your way around?

I had my friends. We helped each other out a lot. Also, don't be afraid to ask a teacher! They know the school really well most of the time. —Katie, 13

Go to the school a couple of days before school starts. Take a look around so that when the first day comes, you will have a basic idea of where to go. Some schools even have maps. Don't be afraid to ask an older classmate for directions. They'll remember what it was like on the first day of school and will be happy to help. —Katilyn, 15

Be organized and prepared! See if you can find a couple of friends that are in your next class and work together to find your class! You can also pray! God is ALWAYS there! —Jennifer, 15

> ## What advice do you have about being around older boys in school?

I would say not to be nervous because they are just boys who are dealing with issues too. Just be yourself, and you may end up making some great guy friends. —Cayla, 14

Unless they want to sincerely be your friend, I would steer clear of older guys in middle school. Not that you have to be afraid of them, you probably won't have many classes with them so you won't have to really deal with them. But if you want to keep your life a lot less complicated, just don't even worry about the older guys. —Alicia, 17

Believe it or not, for most middle schoolers (at the beginning) guys are still—almost—in that "cootie" stage. So things go pretty slow at first, which I say is great. Just remember, you're only in middle school. You have your whole life. Just take it slow, and don't do anything you'll regret. —Leah, 14

Relax. They are just like the boys your age, only taller, and a bit smarter. —Annie, 14

What one piece of advice would you give a girl entering middle school?

Have fun, enjoy it. Don't worry about having a boyfriend. Middle school relationships don't last long and add a lot of unneeded drama and such. Forgive your friend if she made a mistake. You don't wanna lose an awesome friend over silly fights. —Katie, 13

Try hard! And get involved! You won't regret it; you meet so many cool people. And don't just stick to one group of friends. Get out there and meet people. You'll regret not meeting a lot of people. —Sarah, 14

Just be yourself. Don't let the people that you hang out with rub off on you and change you. You are unique because God made you in his image. —Annie, 14

Stay close to God. He will always be a friend you can turn to! These years are very important in deciding who you will be as an adult. Choose friends who will help you do what is right! —Stephanie, 18

Pray a lot. Your prayer time will need to be stable once you enter high school. —Kaitlyn, 16

Be YOURSELF; if you want people to like you and be your friend for WHO YOU ARE, you can't act all the time! —Maria, 14

Boys can sometimes be intimidating, but they are not everything. There is no reason to be "All" about boys. In the Bible it doesn't talk about dating. It just simply talks about finding your future husband. So, girls, unless you plan on getting married soon (I hope you are not!), you can focus more on being true friends without being any more. The world may tell you that you HAVE to have a boyfriend, but that is not true! —Jennifer, 15

Don't stress! You're learning! I made my 1st C on my report card in middle school. You're learning, and if you make mistakes along the way, don't get all bent out of shape about it! Just DO YOUR BEST! —April, 14

Guys in middle school are crazy; they haven't matured yet so they're still in their I DON'T WANT TO GROW UP stage. But, they take a lot of interest in girls at this age. All I want to say is ignore them! They may look all cute and sweet but they are in middle school and you are too young to start thinking about it. Later you will regret it. —Alli, 14

I would just advise you to be yourself! Don't try to be anything you're not! Especially if you're just trying to attract "popular" friends or boys! If they don't like you when you're just yourself, then they aren't even worth the trouble! Just remember Romans 12:2 that tells us not to conform! God made you a unique person who he loves, not some "robot" who is just like everybody else! —Emily, 16

Don't conform to this world. Right now, in middle school, is the time that you are deciding who you are going to be, and what your reputation will be, all throughout your high school years. Stick with Jesus! —Morgan, 15

Never fade in your faith. I know when I went to middle school, the freedom that I had was a little too much. I was cursing and probably not making the best choices. It wasn't until a year or so ago when I really knew I was being stupid. Never forget about God, because he NEVER forgets about you. —Leah, 14

Modest is always hottest. The way you dress determines the kind of attention you get. You'll be tempted at times to dress like the in crowd. Don't. God will bless you and your husband will appreciate it in the long run. You can still be cute and modest. Always try to live so others will see Christ in you. —Elizabeth, 14

My biggest piece of advice is to never let anyone change you. There are so many pressures in middle school to do things that will get you accepted, but those things are not always healthy and are usually not the things that God delights in. Guard your heard and your mind by reading the Bible and don't be afraid to call out to God when being set apart for him seems too much to bear. You are unique because the Father created you to be that way. Don't let anyone tell you otherwise and don't let your peers rob you of your identity in Christ. —Alicia, 17

God is your BEST FRIEND! Talk to him; learn about who he is through his word and tell him everything that goes on during your day. Just like a earthly friend, he loves hearing from you! Lastly, DO NOT get caught up with boys. God will bring you the right one and he will be worth the wait. God wants you to build your character first before you are ready for that job! So BE CONTENT! —Christy, 15 ✳

Live so others can see Christ in you. Don't conform to this world. Stay close to God. He will always be a friend you can turn to.

YOU'VE GOT MAIL!!

God's Letters Reveal How He Feels about You!

I'll give you peace, so don't let your heart be upset or afraid. (see John 14:27)

I demonstrated my radical true-friend love by laying down my life for you. (see John 15:13—15)

I've shown kindness by giving you rain, plenty of food, and a joyful heart. (see Acts 14:17)

I'll soon crush that enemy Satan under your feet. (see Romans 16:20)

I'll make sure you have what you need for every good work. (see 2 Corinthians 9:8)

My grace will get you through anything, and my power shows up best in your weakness. (see 2 Corinthians 12:7—10)

I've already set you free and you're the only one who can change that. (see Galatians 5:1)

You can do all things in my strength. (see Philippians 4:13)

I'll meet all your needs with my fabulous riches. (see Philippians 4:19)

I constantly strengthen and protect you from the evil one. (see 2 Thessalonians 3:3)

Even if you are faithless to me, I will remain faithful to you. (see 2 Timothy 2:13)

I was tempted in every way, so I can help when you are tempted. (see Hebrews 2:18)

Faith is the only way to please me. Believe me, seek me to the extreme, and I will reward you. (see Hebrews 11:6)

Come close to me, and I'll come close to you. (see James 4:8)

I'm not slow in keeping my promises; I'm patient so that everyone you know has a chance to believe. (see 2 Peter 3:9)

I'm coming soon! I'll give everyone what they deserve, so be ready. (see Revelation 22:12—13)

Isn't this stuff amazing?!

Chapter 2:
Faith

a Leap of Faith

by Susie Davis

A couple of weeks ago, my family and I visited Camp Timberline in Estes Park, Colorado, where our son, Will, had just finished his summer term as a counselor. Besides being a counselor to the kids, he also was in charge of the ropes course. I don't know how much you know about a ropes course, but I can tell you what I thought when I saw them . . . they look a lot like something Tarzan might have left in the jungle after a long day playing with the monkeys. There are all these ropes stretched from one tree to another high in the air. And the campers like to come to the ropes course and climb way up high into the trees, attach themselves to one of the ropes, and swing out over the open ground, zipping along like a flying squirrel. Seems kinda crazy to me, but Will says all the campers love it.

There is one part of the ropes course called "The Leap of Faith." In this part of the course, a camper climbs a pole, which is just like a telephone pole but way more wobbly. And then they stand at the top of it with their toes hanging off because it's only about ten inches wide. The camper is supposed to jump off the pole and try to catch a swinging trapeze bar, like at the circus but with no net underneath. Scary!

Now, just to let you know, all the campers have to wear a harness fitted around their legs and waist and this harness is attached with a rope to a metal line above them just in case they miss the swing. So really there's no fear of a kid smashing into the ground below when the harness is safely attached. (Thank goodness.) But even though it's completely safe, most of the campers are still nervous when they climb the pole because it's really high up there. They carefully stand on the top of the skinny pole and look down anxiously because they feel afraid. (I can certainly understand that!) As a matter of fact, some of the campers feel so nervous they change their mind about jumping off. But there's one little problem: A camp rule states that once you're atop the pole, the only way down is to jump out to the swing. Yikes!

My son Will told me most campers wonder about their safety when they are finally up there. He says a lot of the campers wonder out loud that maybe the rope won't hold them. They get freaked out thinking about how horrible it would be if they smashed into the hard ground thirty feet below. As a matter of fact, Will says the scariest part for the campers is that they have to trust the rope attached to their back through the harness. But because they can't see the rope and they can't feel the rope, they worry that the rope won't be there to save them if they miss the swing.

> # Becoming a Christian is a daring thing to do because we can't see God and we can't feel God. It takes faith to believe in God.

I have to confess, when I saw all those ropes high in the air, I felt afraid just thinking about climbing up there. I certainly didn't want to give "The Leap of Faith" a try. Jumping out thirty feet over the ground, free falling through the air to try and catch the trapeze swing, just sounds a little too risky to me. I think you have to be pretty brave to try something like that.

Now, while I'm not likely to try "The Leap of Faith" any time soon, there is something else I did that I think is quite brave. It's not in the fun and games department of my life; rather, it's in the spiritual part of my life. I became a Christian. And I believe becoming a Christian is a brave thing to do. Because if you think about it, God asks us to do something bold when he asks us to believe in him with all our heart. Becoming a Christian is a daring thing to do because we can't see God and we can't feel God. It takes faith to believe in God.

Hebrews 11:1 defines faith like this: "Now faith is being sure of what we hope for and certain of what we do not see" (NIV). See, faith itself is about believing in something you can't see with your eyes and being a Christian requires faith. Hebrews 11: 6 says this, "It's impossible to please God apart from faith. And why? Because anyone who wants to approach God must believe both that he exists and that he cares enough to respond to those who seek him" *(The Message)*. Becoming a Christian is taking your heart and jumping out to God even though you can't see him and even though you can't feel him.

In a small way, it's like what the kids did with their bodies when they were on the high ropes.

> Becoming a Christian is taking your heart and jumping out to God even though you can't see him or feel him.

They could say they trusted that rope to catch them if they fell but until they were able to get brave and jump out there toward the swing, they weren't believing the rope would catch them. As long as they stood scared and confused on top of the pole, they weren't giving the rope a chance to do its job.

And it is the same with our faith in God. We can talk all about Jesus—but until we make a decision to believe who he says he is in the Bible and give him our whole hearts in faith, we don't really trust him yet.

When you pray to Jesus, though you have never seen him, and accept that he is God's Son sent to die for you, that is when you are able to have faith. And that is the one thing God is most interested in you doing. John 3:16–18 says this:

"God loved the people of this world so much that he gave his only Son, so that everyone who has faith in him will have eternal life and never really die. God did not send his Son into the world to condemn its people. He sent him to save them! No one who has faith in God's Son will be condemned" (CEV).

Are you ready to take your heart and jump out to God? Are you ready to pray to God and become a Christian? It's a brave thing to do. And even though it might seem a little scary, you need to know that God is way more able to catch you than a harnessed high rope. He will be there for you!

*See "Are You Running the Right Race?" on page 80 to learn more about making a decision to follow Christ and become a Christian! *

JUST BETWEEN US

1. Can you think of a time when you had to rely on faith to get you through something?

2. What makes it hard to have faith?

3. Why is faith important?

JESUS:
Man or Messiah?

Let's say you're totally good at guessing. One day you hear there's a new girl coming to school, so just for fun you talk your friends into having a friendly little contest to see who can guess the most accurate information about her.

And hey, no contest is complete without a great prize, so you all chip in for the winner to receive a double-scoop of Mega Brownie Madness down at Happy Harley's Ice Cream Shop.

The rules are set. Everyone has to guess eight random things about the new chick, write them down on paper, and turn them in to the group. Your list looks like this:

- **A girl named Roxy**
- **Mr. Fridley's granddaughter**
- **Moving from Lost Creek, West Virginia**
- **Moving into the house on Buzzard Road**
- **Parents' names are Ralph and Inga Fridley**
- **Has a pet iguana named "Spike"**
- **Collects wacky key chains**
- **Went to Disney World for her tenth birthday**

Finally she shows up and you and your friends rush to find her at lunch to get better acquainted. No one can believe it when you get every single guess right. In fact, all your friends get mad and blame you for cheating. But you're still happy because you get your favorite ice cream.

54   between us girls ✳ faith

OK, that's pretty far out, but there's a point. It's obvious that nobody could be that good at guessing, right? You'd have to be as smart as God! He's the only one who knows everything. For instance, in the Bible God told us lots of specific things about a certain person hundreds of years before he ever lived on the earth—before anyone could even make a guess—called prophecies. Yep, before his Son Jesus was even born, way back in the days of Old Testament dudes, God told us all about Jesus so we'd recognize him when he came to Earth.

Get this. We were told things like: he'd be born from a virgin, a descendant of Abraham and David, be born in Bethlehem,

> ... the probability of eight prophecies coming true in one person is only one chance in 100,000,000,000,000,000.

grow up in Nazareth, ride a donkey into Jerusalem, be betrayed by a friend for thirty pieces of silver, be crucified, and have no bones broken at his death. There you go, eight fulfilled prophecies.

Now I'm no math expert, but thankfully there are fancy scientists out there who actually enjoy calculating the chance of something like this happening. These math showoffs, down at the American Scientific Affiliation, claim that the probability of eight prophecies coming true in one person is only one chance in 100,000,000,000,000,000. Whoa, that's a big number! Sort of mind-boggling.

Josh McDowell, a famous youth speaker explains this number for people like me who

**WOW . . .
with odds like that, God seems so much bigger and more amazing than ever!**

are a little slow getting it in real people terms. "Take the huge state of Texas and fill the entire state two feet deep with silver dollars. Then take one silver dollar, mark it with a big red X, and toss it somewhere back into the pile. Then, blindfold someone, and let her walk all over Texas and pick up one single silver dollar out of that two-foot-deep pile. The chance that, on her first attempt she found the silver dollar marked with the red X, is the same likelihood that just eight of these prophecies could be fulfilled in any one individual!"[1]

As if that isn't impressive enough, way more than eight (more like sixty) detailed Bible prophecies all came true years later about Jesus. Wow . . . with odds like that, God seems so much bigger and more amazing than ever! To think that he gave so many prophecies about his Son so many years before and they all came true. Now that's one way-smart and positively cool God! ✳

_____

1. Josh McDowell, *Beyond Belief to Convictions* (Tyndale House Publishers, 2002).

JUST BETWEEN US

1. **What is a prophecy?**

2. **Why is it important that Jesus fulfilled all the prophecies written about him in the Bible?**

3. **How can Jesus' fulfillment of the prophecies help us to trust God?**

YOU'VE GOT MAIL!!

by Julie Ferwerda

God's Letters Reveal His sweet personality

Did you know different books of the Bible highlight different parts of God's personality? Match God's awesome character quality on the right with the correct Scripture at the left. (For use with NIV.)

1. Genesis 1: 1-31
2. Exodus 3:28
3. Deuteronomy 6:23; 28:9
4. Psalms 23:4; 118:7
5. Proverbs 2:1-5
6. Isaiah 40:1; 66:13
7. Jeremiah 18:1-6
8. Daniel 3:27-28; 6:21-24
9. Matthew 1:23
10. Luke 5:32; 15:2
11. John 1:4-5; 8:12
12. Romans 8:1
13. 2 Corinthians 8:9; 9:10-11
14. Galatians 5:1; 5:13
15. Ephesians 2:4-6
16. Philippians 1:25-26; 4:4
17. 2 Thessalonians 3:3
18. Hebrews 4:15
19. 1 John 4:8-10
20. Revelation 19:11-16

a. Joy-giver
b. Faithful God
c. Understands your struggles
d. left heaven to live with his people
e. Generous
f. Compassionate comforter
g. Freedom-Giver
h. Knight in Shining armor (Rescuer)
i. Wise counselor
j. Brave and strong warrior
k. Life-giver
l. Amazing Creator
m. Clean-slate forgiver
n. True love
o. BFF & helper
p. Promise keeper
q. Friend of sinners
r. Light of the world
s. Fierce protector
t. Perfect potter

Answers: 1-L; 2-H; 3-P; 4-O; 5-I; 6-F; 7-T; 8-S; 9-D; 10-Q; 11-R; 12-M; 13-E; 14-G; 15-K; 16-A; 17-B; 18-C; 19-N; 20-J

creative ways

When I was growing up, we only had a few ways to communicate with people: face-to-face conversation, letter in the mail, or phone call on a home telephone.

I know, I know, it's hard to imagine a world without cell phones and computers! Somehow we survived.

Today there are a gazillion other ways to communicate with people: text messaging, instant messaging, online chatting, and e-mailing to name a few. Just as there are options when communicating with each other, the same is true of God. Prayer is one approach, but there are also lots of other ways to creatively connect with our Father. No laptop required!

Let them praise his name with dancing and make music to him with tambourine and harp. (Psalm 149:3 NIV)

Start by picking an activity that you naturally like to do, such as singing or painting. Then think of a way that you can praise God by doing that activity. For the artist, maybe it's painting things you see outside that remind you God is the ultimate Creator (skies, mountains, flowers, etc). For the singer, maybe it's singing praise songs when you're in the shower. (A little *American Idol* practice, perhaps?)

Here are some other ideas for you creative types:

If drawing's your thing:

- Make a "thank you" card to God and draw the things that you are grateful for in your life.
- Create a poster/sign and write this sentence at the top—"I am happy that God made me the way I am" or "I am fearfully and wonderfully made" and then draw unique things about yourself that God created (your talents, your physical features, etc.).

If writing's your thing:

- Write in a journal the top ten reasons that you love God.
- List words describing God starting with each letter of the alphabet.
- Write about a Bible story as if you were one of the characters (what you may have felt, heard, or seen). For example, you could write from Jonah's perspective when he was in the belly of the whale!

If scrapbooking's your thing:

- Cut out words from a magazine that describe how you view God (for example: friend, father, love, wonderful, etc.). Then, create a page with those words, and put a picture of you in the middle to

to connect with God

by Susan Jones

show how God surrounds you in his love.
- Make a page filled with pictures of friends or family who don't know God yet. Then, pray for them!
- Create a page with your favorite Bible verse and decorate it! (Verses work really well as borders too!)

If dancing's your thing:
- Make up a dance to your favorite praise song. Then dance for him. (Don't worry, no one is watching.)
- Create a dance to represent the different days of creation. See "That's Wild" on page 102, or read **Genesis 1** to find out what God created each day.
- Dress up as a princess and create a ballet dance where you dance before God the King.

If crafts are your thing:
- Create a piece of art that reminds you of God. Maybe you make a Popsicle stick cross, or decorate a flower pot that reminds you to be growing in your faith! **(see Luke 2:52).**

- Make a bookmark with your favorite Bible verse on it.
- Make a crown to remind yourself that you are a princess in God's kingdom!
- Decorate a box, or other item, and use it to begin collecting your pennies or coins to give to a local charity. Jesus tells us to take care of the poor!

If poetry's your thing:
- Write a poem that tells the story of your love for him. (Rhyming is not required!)
- Write a poem describing what you hope heaven is like.

If singing's your thing:
- Make up a song to your favorite verse in the Bible. Try looking in **Psalms** for some lyrics.

If beading's your thing:
- Make a bracelet with beads to represent the fruits of the spirit **(see Galatians 5:22-23).** *

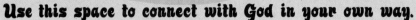

Use this space to connect with God in your own way.

JUST BETWEEN US

1. What other ways can you think of to creatively connect with God?

2. How do you like to communicate with God? Why?

3. Why do you think it's important to communicate with him?

What's God Like?

by Susan Jones

Word Scramble

Unscramble the words on the left to learn about the unique personality of God! Then match up the words with their definitions on the right. If you need help, turn to the Scripture reference in your Bible. (See "Dig into God's Word" on page 98 for help finding books of the Bible.) ✳

God is . . .

1. **DINK** _____
   (Titus 3:4)

2. **NGLOIV** _____
   (1 John 4:7–8; Psalm 25:10)

3. **HAFILUTF** _____
   (Psalm 33:4; Psalm 36:5)

4. **WFEPROLU** _____
   (Psalm 77:13–14; Psalm 89:13; Psalm 145:6)

5. **HWEEVRYEER** _____
   (Psalm 139:7–12)

6. **SIEW** _____
   (Romans 6:27)

7. **YLHO** _____
   (Psalm 99:3–5)

8. **AUCHNGGINN** _____
   (Malachi 3:6)

9. **UTTRH** _____
   (John 14:6)

10. **ULMICERF** _____
    (Ephesians 2:4)

a. not changing or capable of change; constant

b. showing a kind and gentle treatment of someone (as a wrongdoer or opponent) having no right to it; having compassion

c. wanting and liking to do good and to bring happiness to others; showing or growing out of gentleness or goodness of heart

d. full of influence; strong

e. the quality or state of being true; real

f. worthy of complete devotion and trust; set apart to the service of God

g. feeling or showing love; affectionate

h. good sense, or good judgment, sensible

i. in every place

j. loyal; firm in keeping promises or in fulfilling duties; true to the facts

Answers for scrambled words:
1-kind // 2-loving // 3-faithful // 4-powerful // 5-everywhere // 6-wise // 7-holy // 8-unchanging // 9-truth // 10-merciful

Answers:
1-c // 2-g // 3-j // 4-d // 5-i // 6-h // 7-f // 8-a // 9-e // 10-b

Mud, A Very Faithful Dog

by Susan Jones

Imagine the cutest dog you've ever seen. Now imagine an even cuter dog, and you've got Mud. Mud is a very large, brown, very cute chocolate Labrador retriever, and he weighs about 95 pounds! That's probably more than you!

Mud is a great dog. He loves the water, likes to be petted, and, like most dogs, loves to sleep! Sometimes I think he's dead because he sleeps so much.☺ There are a lot of things I love about Mud, like the way he follows me around the house or his "I'm guilty" look when he's caught digging in the trash. But my favorite thing about Mud is that I can count on him to love me.

A few years ago my best friend in the world stopped being my friend. It happened suddenly, and I had no idea why we weren't friends anymore. My feelings were hurt so bad that I went through many tissue boxes crying over this loss. In my sadness, sweet Mud would literally lick tears right off my cheek! I'm sure it's just because they were salty, but I like to think he was giving me comfort, whether he meant to or not.

During that hard time, every day when I came home, big, brown Mud would greet me with a wagging tail and smiley eyes. Sure, he was just a dog, but he was also my friend. This happened time and time again, even on days when I didn't pay much attention to Mud.

Sometimes I would be gone all day, and make it home just before bedtime. But, Mud still loved me. Then there were times when I had friends over, and I had to put Mud in the backyard away from everyone. (Hard to believe some people didn't want chocolate lab love, isn't it?) Still, sometimes he got in the way a little, so outside he went. But, Mud still loved me. And every now and then I would leave to go out of town for a few days, and leave Mud in the yard for people to come over and feed him once a day. But, Mud still loved me. No matter how many times I was unable to give him the love and attention he deserved, he loved me. He never failed to greet me with love and affection, a wagging tail, and smiley eyes. He faithfully loved me.

Hmm . . . that sounds a lot like someone else I know.

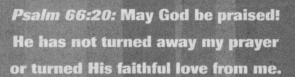

there is only One who is faithful above all others . . . God.

There is only One who is faithful above all others . . . God. The Bible is filled with verses about God's faithfulness toward us. Here are just a few:

Psalm 59:17: **To You, my strength, I sing praises, because God is my stronghold—my faithful God.**

Psalm 89:8: **LORD God of Hosts, who is strong like You, LORD? Your faithfulness surrounds You.**

Psalm 66:20: **May God be praised! He has not turned away my prayer or turned His faithful love from me.**

What's so great about God's faithfulness? Well, it means that no matter what, God has promised to love us. You know how sometimes people let us down, and break their promises? God's not like that. In fact, he can't be unfaithful. It's totally opposite of who he is. He's the best promise-keeper around, and he's promised to love us!

Even though we try hard, we will never be fully faithful to God. Unfortunately we all sin, or mess up. Happens all the time. A little attitude to the parents, a hint of jealousy when a football star brother gets more attention than we do, or a dab of selfishness when asked to share the remote with a little sister. But how cool is it that God was faithful to send his Son, Jesus, to forgive those nasty sins?! God even takes it a step further because the Bible

no matter what, God has promised to love us.

says that he is faithful to help us when we are simply tempted to sin! (1 Corinthians 10:13). Whoa! Now that's faithfulness!

Nothing we can do will separate us from the love of God. Even when we mess up, or blow him off, God is still faithful to tenderly forgive us and eagerly waits to greet us. And, while I'm sure he doesn't have a wagging tail, I bet he has smiley eyes.✻

PS: Dog is God spelled backward . . . coincidence? I think not!

JUST BETWEEN US

Nothing we can do will separate us from the love of God!

1. Why is faithfulness important in relationships?

2. How does God's faithfulness toward you make you feel? Why?

3. How can we be faithful to God?

10

SUPER COOL THINGS *about:*

Heaven

by Julie Ferwerda

1. You'll get to hang out having fun with God in person every day. (Revelation 21:3)

2. You'll get a brand new stunning version of the body you live in now. (1 Corinthians 15:40)

3. You'll never be sick, sad, or in pain. (Revelation 21:4)

4. You'll get to live on a brand new Earth that's way better. (2 Peter 3:13)

5. You'll hang out with millions of angels who will probably have some great behind-the-scenes stories to tell you from your life. (Revelation 5:11)

6. You'll get to live in a positively spectacular house. (John 14:2)

7. Animals will live there with you. (Isaiah 65:25)

8. You'll get to eat amazing food. Whoa yeah! (Revelation 19:9)

9. You can splash and play in rivers. (Revelation 22:1)

10. Jesus will be King in an awesome city called The New Jerusalem with pearls for gates and gold streets. (Revelation 21:2)✻

Lighten up!
Discover
the Bright Side of God
In Your Own Backyard

by Julie Ferwerda

Every now and then I'm walking along, minding my own business, when I happen to notice something around me on this amazing planet that's a little bit like God. It's like he's left these little clues all over this world just so I can learn more about him. Sometimes it's such an obvious thing like something I've seen a thousand times already but never really noticed it, and I feel like such a doofus for being so clueless. That's exactly what happened last Thursday . . .

It all started when I was outside in my backyard, staring off into space—one of my favorite summer activities—when I noticed the sunlight shining and gleaming all over everything, like the sun is famous for doing. I noticed this because it was so bright; I had to actually get up to get my jazzy new shades. All this got me thinking about the amazing qualities I've noticed about sunlight during my short, yet observant, life. Here are some of the thoughts I had about sunlight:

◎ Gives super-growing power.
Sunlight makes tiny seeds grow up into things like strong monkey-swinging, kid-climbing, panda-munching trees.

Helps us find our way around.

That's great news for people (like me) who get freaked out in the pitch dark recesses of batty caves and spider-infested basements. I'll stay out in the light of day, thank you very much.

Wins 100 percent over darkness.

Want to see a really cool disappearing act? Go into a totally dark room, close the door, and turn on a light. What happens to the dark? For added fun, try this trick out on your friends.

Leaves a lasting effect.

It makes even my lily-white skin turn a nice shade of pink while basking in my backyard.

Can't be seen.

Weirdly, you can't actually see light; you can only see what it touches! Light is shining 24/7 (thankfully no one has figured out how to turn off the sun yet), zooming right past the earth in all that outer space we can see at night, but we don't see it because it's not touching anything except the bright, shiny, reflective moon.

Shines out forever.

Although no one knows this for sure, many light experts believe that once light leaves the sun, it keeps going forever or until something intercepts it.

Makes the world a happier place.

For real! How many times have you seen a happy sunflower growing in the dark, or noticed gorgeous sparkly snowbanks at night?

That's all positively cool stuff because, in the Bible, God calls himself "light." That means he's trying to teach us something about his nature through sunbeams. For instance, he's eternal, of course. And though he's invisible, you can see the things he touches . . . like his amazingly colorful sunsets, or like when he helps you find your way through a rough and confusing time.

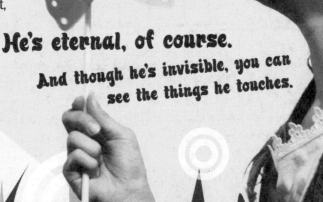

He's eternal, of course.
And though he's invisible, you can see the things he touches.

Basking in his Word and talking to him throughout my day sure makes me a noticeably nicer person to be around. Planting his seeds of love, I get to watch him do the magic of growing me into a completely changed person, strong in faith and character. All his beauty shining out every day lights up the whole world, making my life a brighter and happier place!

Wow, go figure. Who'd ever guess you could get all of that out of one afternoon staring at your backyard? Maybe there are other simple hints scattered all around my world every day that could teach me even more about God. I'll just have to pay attention so I don't miss them! For now, I think I'll grab my jazzy shades, some cold lemonade, and head out to work on my tan, with plenty of sunscreen, of course!✳

Though he's invisible, you can see the things he touches.

JUST BETWEEN US

1. Name some things that you use light for and why light is important in your life. Why is God important in your life?

2. What's something else in nature that reminds you of God? Why?

3. Why do you suppose things in nature remind us of God?

HELLO MY NAME IS

God

the name game

by Susan Jones

If you were asked to introduce yourself, you'd probably say, "Hello, my name is ____." What if someone asked you to describe yourself? You might start naming different roles in your life. For example, you might say, "I'm in fourth grade, I play soccer, and I have two brothers." Basically, you've just described yourself as a student, an athlete, and a sister. There are a lot of different ways to show who you are.

The same is true of God! He goes by many different names in the Bible based on all sorts of "roles" that he plays. Same God; different names. The different names help to describe God in all his awesomeness so we can have a bigger picture of his character and personality!

Try matching these different names of God with their descriptions. Then, write in the last column how each description of God affects your life.

Descriptions	Name of God	That's important to me because...
a. The Lord Heals	1. Jehovah Jirah *(hint: gives)*	
b. The Everlasting God	2. El Shaddai *(hint: strong)*	
c. The Lord is Peace	3. El Roi *(hint: eyes)*	
d. The Lord Most High	4. Adonai *(hint: obey)*	
e. The Lord Will Provide	5. Jehovah-Ra'ah *(hint: sheep)*	
f. The God who sees	6. El Olam *(hint: forever)*	
g. The Lord Almighty	7. El Elyon *(hint: above)*	
h. The Lord is present	8. Jehovah-Shalom *(hint: dove)*	
i. Master	9. Jehovah-Rapha *(hint: ouch!)*	
j. The Lord our Shepherd	10. Jehovah-Shammah *(hint: here & now)*	

Answers: 1=e // 2=g // 3=f // 4=i // 5=j // 6=b // 7=d // 8=c // 9=a // 10=h

The Small Answer to the BIG QUESTION: Why Do Bad Things Happen

by Susie Davis

Something happened to me when I was fourteen that changed my life. It wasn't making cheerleader. It wasn't discovering a talent for singing that would lead me to compete on *American Idol*. No, it wasn't anything like that at all. Instead what happened to me led to years of asking a hard question over and over again: *Why do bad things happen?* It is a question that I have begged God to answer. And honestly, in some ways I still struggle with understanding it.

A little history: When I was in junior high, my favorite teacher died suddenly and unexpectedly. One day he was teaching English class and the next day he wasn't. I remember the feeling that I had when I realized I would never see him again. It was as if someone had socked me in the stomach hard—so hard that I felt like I couldn't catch my breath. No one was expecting his death so it came as a real shock to me and the other kids in my class. We missed him and wanted just one more chance to see him again, but he was gone.

Maybe you have had a similar situation. Perhaps you've had a grandparent die. Or maybe you have a friend whose mom or dad suffered with cancer. Those kinds of situations sometimes happen and when they do, it can bring up a lot of questions.

Many of the choices people make are the wrong ones.

It certainly did for me because although I was a Christian at the time my teacher died, I still had a ton of sad and confusing feelings. I wondered why God would let someone die like that so unexpectedly. And then I began to look at all the bad things that happen in the world around me and ask the hard question: *Why do bad things happen?* It made me feel lonely and hopeless inside.

As I grew and learned more about God and the Bible, I came to understand that bad things happen in the world because God gives us the ability to make choices for ourselves. The very beginning of "bad things" actually started in the Garden of Eden when Adam and Eve made a wrong choice that God calls sin. Sin was the beginning of death as we know it.

Sin makes people feel sad and confused. It makes people feel hurt and hopeless. But that's what sin does. Sin is just a part of what happened when God gave us the freedom to make choices for ourselves. But another thing I learned as I grew is that the hopelessness of sin is not a part of what God wants for me or for you.

There is a verse in Romans 5:20 and it says, "Yet where sin was powerful, God's kindness was even more powerful" (CEV). The Bible is promising that even though sin is horrible and it breaks people's hearts—God's kindness is more powerful.

God gave us the freedom to make **choices** for ourselves.

God's kindness is Jesus. When God sent Jesus to deal with the sin and pain problem, his love and kindness became the king of everything. God did not leave us without hope or without comfort in horrible times. Instead, he gave us Jesus as the final say on any doubts we might have about God's goodness and his love.

Now, you need to know this. Even though you know sin is the reason why bad things happen, I have to tell you something. When I was trying to understand the whole idea of death and why people we love die, knowing the Bible's answer to all the questions didn't help me feel a lot better right away.

As a matter of fact, I still missed my teacher for some time after he died. That's really pretty normal. And it's good to talk about those kinds of feelings. I would also encourage you to talk to your Mom or Dad if you have questions about why bad things happen in life. They can help you through times that seem sad and confusing. They can pray with you and hug on you, helping you see just how big God's kindness can be. ✳

I had a lot of UNANSWERED Questions

JUST ♥ BETWEEN ♥ US

1. **When something bad happens in your life, what gets you through it?**

2. **How can God be a comfort during those times?**

3. **What can you do to prepare for tough times?**

Really BIG Words

by Susan Jones

crossword puzzle

ACROSS

1. Someone who says one thing but does another
3. When God became man (Jesus)
7. To turn away from sin
10. God knows everything
11. Regular check-ins with a friend to help each other stay focused on doing the right things
12. God is all-powerful
13. God is everywhere all the time

DOWN

2. To pay a price for something; when Jesus paid the price for our sins by dying on the cross
4. Being pure and clean in God's sight
5. Sharing the good news about Christ
6. The act of our sins being cleansed away forever! It happens the minute we receive Jesus
8. A Christian, or student of Christ
9. Swearing using God's name or saying bad things about God

>>**Answers on page 75!** ✱

Need some help?
Here's a word bank:

Omniscience   Omnipresent   Hypocrite   Repentance   Redemption
Omnipotent   Incarnation   Righteousness   Evangelism   Disciple
Justification   Blasphemy   Accountability

Quiz

Fact or Fiction

by Julie Ferwerda

How do you rate on these faith facts? Answer T or F.

1. ___ Christianity is all about a bunch of rules to follow.

2. ___ Dinosaurs and people lived together on the earth.

3. ___ My great- great- great- great- granddaddy was an ape.

4. ___ Heaven is floating out in the cosmos somewhere and when I get there, I might sit around on clouds, playing a harp.

5. ___ In heaven I'll be a floating spirit without a physical body.

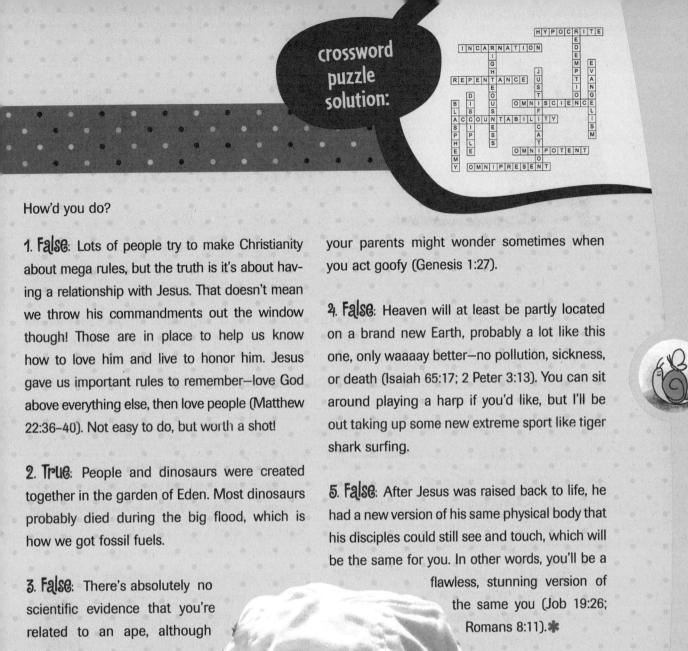

crossword
puzzle
solution:

How'd you do?

1. False: Lots of people try to make Christianity about mega rules, but the truth is it's about having a relationship with Jesus. That doesn't mean we throw his commandments out the window though! Those are in place to help us know how to love him and live to honor him. Jesus gave us important rules to remember—love God above everything else, then love people (Matthew 22:36–40). Not easy to do, but worth a shot!

2. True: People and dinosaurs were created together in the garden of Eden. Most dinosaurs probably died during the big flood, which is how we got fossil fuels.

3. False: There's absolutely no scientific evidence that you're related to an ape, although your parents might wonder sometimes when you act goofy (Genesis 1:27).

4. False: Heaven will at least be partly located on a brand new Earth, probably a lot like this one, only waaaay better—no pollution, sickness, or death (Isaiah 65:17; 2 Peter 3:13). You can sit around playing a harp if you'd like, but I'll be out taking up some new extreme sport like tiger shark surfing.

5. False: After Jesus was raised back to life, he had a new version of his same physical body that his disciples could still see and touch, which will be the same for you. In other words, you'll be a flawless, stunning version of the same you (Job 19:26; Romans 8:11). ✳

Squeakers was almost Dessert

by Julie Ferwerda

To say that Squeakers had a bad day would be a big-time understatement! Squeakers is my pet gerbil, and his horrible day all started when I left him home alone with my mouse-loving cat—mouse-loving as in "I-love-eating-chocolate-cake" kind of way. Mental note: never leave my defenseless pet gerbil home alone with my hungry cat. I guess it would have been OK if Squeakers's cage didn't have a hole big enough for a cat's paw to reach inside.

When I got home, I turned on the light and walked through the living room. "Hey, Morty," I greeted my drooling cat. If I'd been paying attention, I would have noticed he looked as guilty as a bear caught stealing honey. "Hi there, Squeakers," I walked by my furry rodent, who was obviously paralyzed with fear. His beady little eyes were trying to tell me something, but I was clueless. Sometimes I can be a little slow.

And then it hit me.

"SQUEAKERS! What are you doing out of your cage? You could get killed pulling a stunt like that!" I couldn't believe he wasn't in gerbil heaven already. After all, this is a professional and ferocious mouse killer we're dealing with here. I quickly scooped him up and, other than being covered in a bunch of cat saliva and a little cut on his eyelid, he seemed to be OK. Putting him back in his cage, I could only imagine what he must have lived through that night. Two hours of being a cat play-toy—knowing you're going to be dessert eventually—would be a very bad day.

Another Cat and Mouse Story

Disobeying God (and your parents) is a lot like this Squeakers story. With the help of your parents, God has created a safe place for you to grow up by putting some rules and boundaries in place. Sometimes rules can seem like a pain, but they're actually the way your heart, body, and future are protected from danger. When you disobey the rules, you allow holes to open up in your safe place that can turn you into hungry-cat food.

So who's the cat? The Bible says that

Satan is like a hungry lion looking for someone to eat. He patiently waits for the right opportunities to get at you and make you his play toy—one he wants to eat later for dessert. How does he do that? First, he injures your trust in God and your good relationship with your parents by telling you lies. One of his favorite lies is that you don't have to listen to God or your parents because they don't know what's best for you. When you quit listening to God and get suckered in by Satan's lies, he slowly eats up the good life and future God has planned for you. If he gets you to believe enough lies, he can ruin your life.

Squeakers was really lucky that night and didn't get gobbled up. He was happy to get back into his safe cozy home and stay there. If you want to experience the awesome plans God has for your life, don't listen to Satan—don't become "dessert." Instead, remember what Jesus said in John 10:10 (my version), "A hungry cat named Satan is only there to steal and kill and destroy. Jesus came so you can have real and eternal life, more and better life than you ever dreamed of." Stay safe and secure by obeying God and your parents, and watch your life turn out to be a completely amazing adventure! ✽

JUST ♥ BETWEEN ♥ US

1. Why does Satan want to injure our trust in God?

2. What can help us to be on alert for Satan's lies?

3. Finish these sentences:

a) Listening to God will bring me _____.

b) Listening to Satan will bring me _____.

So you want to share your faith with your pals, but not sure how to get started?

Here are a few tips to steer you in the right direction.

✳ **Prayer is the E in electricity ... the P in power!** Pray first, share second. When the moment of opportunity comes, ask some conversation-openers, like:

1. Do you go to church with your family anywhere?
2. Do you have any special beliefs about God or Jesus?
3. Do you think there's a heaven or hell?
4. When you die, where do you think you'll go?

Thumbs down!! If they don't seem interested, don't push, and don't take it personally—it's God's job to change hearts. Keep praying.

Thumbs up!! If they act interested, move forward with one of these great options:

Un-Cheat Sheet

Simple Tips for Sharing YOUR FAITH

by Julie Ferweda

1. Tell them about Jesus dying on the cross and how he wants to have a personal relationship with them. Explain your story—how you came to believe in Jesus and how he's changed your life and wants to change their lives too, OR:
2. Beforehand, mark or write down a few Bible verses you can read and discuss with them. Some great verses you can choose from are *Romans 6:23, John 14:6, Romans 10:9–10, 1 John 5:11–13, John 5:24, Revelation 3:23, Ephesians 2:8–9,* OR:
3. Tell them there's a great teacher at your church (youth group or Sunday school), friend, or parent who'd be happy to chat more about this and then follow through.

✳ **Emphasize that being a Christian is a lifetime relationship with Jesus—like a BFF—not just a casual momentary event.**

Before moving on, ask some questions to find out if they're ready for the next step:

1. Do you want forgiveness for your sins, friendship with the one true amazing God, and the opportunity to live forever on a brand new earth with him?
2. Do you believe that Jesus died on a cross and rose to life for you?
3. Are you willing to make Jesus the boss of your life?
4. Are you ready to invite Jesus into your life now?

If you start into any of these options and get stumped by their questions, tell them they can talk to someone you know for more help (at home or church), then invite them to visit that person with you as soon as possible. **Way cool, I think you're ready to go!** ✳

Un-Cheat Sheet

by Julie Ferweda

Getting into the groove of a stoked prayer life can take some practice and creativity, but it's really not a special formula or set of rules. Simply put, God is a person and he just wants you to talk to him (and listen) in meaningful ways. He totally cares about everything you do and he's the only One that will be there through every step of your life. Try out these different ideas:

✳ Go for a walk around your neighborhood and pray for friends, relatives, and neighbors.

✳ Turn down the lights, crank up the tunes on your MP3 player, and sing (or pray) to God.

✳ Watch a sunset (or sunrise) and notice how amazing God is. Thank him for his creation.

✳ Write notes to God in a notebook throughout the day or just before you go to bed.

✳ Write out prayers for friends. When God answers, give friends the notes you prayed for them—they'll be so happy and amazed you took that time for them.

✳ Open up Psalms and read random verses of praise you like out loud to God.

✳ Keep a prayer journal on your computer.

✳ Write out things you're thankful for, or answers to prayer, and put them in a special jar (or post on sticky notes somewhere) to read and remember.

✳ Make a prayer bulletin board with photos and notes to remind you who to pray for.

✳ Start a "prayer wall" with friends. Post your requests on paper or poster board and put it where you can all share and pray for each other. Post answers, too.

✳ Doodle special pictures for God.

✳ Start a cell phone prayer hotline for your friends. Offer to pray for/with them anytime.

✳ Take a long bubble bath and talk to God or sing worship songs.

✳ For fun, write a love letter to God, stick it in a balloon, fill it with helium, and send it up.

✳ Close your eyes and visualize your favorite spot—a garden, the beach, or the mountains—and just hang out there with Jesus, talking to him about everyday stuff. ✳

write a love letter to God

Write out things you're thankful for

Are YOU Running the Right Race?

by Vicki Courtney

When I was a little girl, I remember watching the track and field part of the Summer Olympics. I loved watching the winners cross the finish line, pumping their fists in the air as they took their victory lap. First Corinthians 9:24 talks about Christians running in a race. Here is what it says:

> Do you not know that in a race all the runners run, but only one gets the prize? Run in such a way as to get the prize.
>
> 1 Corinthians 9:24 (NIV)

And it got me thinking. **There are basically two races you can enter in this world.** There is the world's race and then there is the Christian race. In the world's race, you run for the crowd. Along the way, you hope to gather up lots and lots of worldly prizes (stuff, money, friends, popularity, etc.). In the Christian race, you run for an audience of one (God!) and try to run in such a way that would be pleasing to God. Along the way, you hope to gather up lots and lots of heavenly prizes (serving others, sharing about Christ, mission trips, reading the Bible, praying, etc.).

In both races, you will someday cross the finish line on the day you die. But here's the problem. **The finish line in the world's race is just that; it's the finish.** You're done. Kaput. Finished. End of the line. The worst part is that you are separated from God forever. No second chance to start over and reenter the Christian race.

In the Christian race, the finish line is not really the finish. In fact, it's kind of like the starting line for an even bigger and better race. When we cross the finish line in the Christian race, we enter the gates of heaven and we spend eternity (forever and

ever) with God. We dwell in the house of the Lord, forever.

There are a couple of Bible verses in Matthew 7:13–14 that make people kind of nervous when they read them, but they are very important verses to know. Here is what they say:

> You can enter God's Kingdom only through the narrow gate. The highway to hell is broad, and its gate is wide for the many who choose that way. But the gateway to life is very narrow, and the road is difficult, and only a few ever find it.
>
> **Matthew 7:13–14 (NLT)**

If you are not quite sure if you are a Christian (in the Christian race), I want you to read what it means to be a Christian on the next page.

Remember, this is the most important decision you will ever make in your life. No one can make this decision for you. You have to make it on your own. Read very carefully and try to understand what each verse means. Don't worry, we'll take it real slow and go step by step.

We Learn about God's Love in the Bible

"For God so loved the world that he gave his one and only Son, that whoever believes in him shall not perish but have eternal life."

John 3:16 (NIV)

God loves you. He wants to bless your life and make it happy, full, and complete. He wants to give you a life that will last forever, even after you die. Perish means to die and to be apart from God—forever. God wants you to have "eternal life" in heaven where you are with him forever. **If you understand what John 3:16 means, put a check here:** ❏

We Are Sinful

For everyone has sinned; we all fall short of God's glorious standard.

Romans 3:23 (NLT)

You may have heard someone say, "I'm only human—nobody's perfect." This Bible verse says the same thing: We are all sinners. No one is perfect. **When we sin, we do things that are wrong—things that God would not agree with.** The verse says we fall short of "God's glorious standard." Imagine that God gives you a test (I know—yuck!). Imagine that you have to make a 100 to meet God's "standard." It makes sense that you have to make a 100 because it's a perfect score and God is perfect. Now let's say that everyone starts with a 100, but anytime you sin (do something wrong), you get a point taken off. Since God is perfect and we are not, it is impossible for anyone to make a 100 on this test! I know it sounds like a strict rule, but think about it. If he is holy and perfect, he can't be around people who are not holy and perfect. If he is, he won't be holy and perfect anymore. **But before you start to worry that you don't meet his standard (you won't make a 100), just wait—there's good news ahead.** **If you understand what Romans 3:23 means, put a check here:** ❏

Sin has a Penalty (Punishment)

> "For the wages (cost) of sin is death."
>
> Romans 6:23 (NIV)

Just as criminals must pay the penalty for their crimes, sinners must pay the penalty for their sins. Imagine this: What if every time we do something wrong, we get a ticket (kind of like if your mom is speeding in her car and gets a ticket and has to pay money for her punishment). Let's also say that our punishment is not that we have to pay money for our sins, but instead, we have to die. When we die, we will be separated from God for all eternity unless there is a way to pay for our sins (which there is, so don't worry—I'll get to that part!). **The Bible teaches that those who choose to be separated from God will spend eternity in a place called hell.** You may have heard some bad things about hell, but the worst part about hell is that you are in a place where you are separated from God forever and ever.
If you understand what Romans 6:23 means, put a check here: ❏

Christ has Paid the Price for Our Sins!

> But God showed his great love for us by sending Christ to die for us while we were still sinners.
>
> Romans 5:8 (NLT)

The Bible teaches that Jesus Christ, the sinless (perfect) Son of God, has paid the price for all your sins. You may think you have to lead a good life and do good deeds before God will love you. It's good to do good deeds, but it won't pay the price for your sins and get you into heaven. The reason is that no matter how many good deeds you do, you still won't have a 100 (be perfect). **But the Bible says that Christ loved you enough to die for you, even when you were acting unlovable. Pretty amazing, huh?!**
If you understand what Romans 5:8 means, put a check here: ❏

Salvation (Life In Heaven) Is a Free Gift

God saved you by his grace
favor when you believed. And
you can't take credit for this;
it is a gift from God.
Salvation is not a reward for
the good things we have done,
so none of us can boast
about it.

Ephesians 2:8–9 (NLT)

The word *grace* means a gift we don't deserve. It means Christ is offering to pay for something you could never pay for yourself: forgiveness of sins and eternal life, **God's gift to you is free. You do not have to work for a gift. That's why it's called a gift.** All you have to do is joyfully receive it. Believe with all your heart that Jesus Christ died for you and paid the price for your sins!

If you understand what Ephesians 2:8–9 means, put a check here: ❏

Christ Is at Your Heart's Door

"Here I am! I stand at the door
and knock. If anyone hears my
voice and opens the door,
I will come in and eat
with him, and he with me."

Revelation 3:20 (NIV)

Jesus Christ wants to have a personal relationship with you. He wants to be your very best friend. He wants you to talk to him just like you would talk to your best friend. Picture, if you will, Jesus Christ standing at the door of your heart and knocking. Invite him in; he is waiting for you to receive him into your heart and life.

If you understand what Revelation 3:20 means, put a check here: ❏

You Must Receive Him

But to all who believed him and
accepted him, he gave the right to
become children of God.

John 1:12 (NLT)

When you receive Christ into your heart you become a child of God, and you can talk to him in prayer at any time about anything. The Christian life is a personal relationship

Way To GO!

(Above was adapted from "Your Christian Life" 1965, 1968, as "Aids to Christian Living," 1986 as "Practical Steps in Christian Living," 1995 as "Beginning Your Christian Life," 1997 as "Your Christian Life," Billy Graham Evangelistic Association.)

(just like you have with your parents or best friend) with God through Jesus Christ. **And best of all, it is a relationship that will last forever and ever. There is nothing you could ever do to make God stop loving you.** Even though we will continue to sin from time to time, God still loves us. He never takes his gift back, so we don't have to worry about losing it. It is ours to keep forever.
If you understand what John 1:12 means, put a check here: ❏

So, what do you think about God's offer of forgiveness? Is this a gift you want to accept? If so, tell God. You don't have to say a fancy prayer—**just talk to him and tell him that you believe that Jesus died on the cross for your sins and you want to accept that gift. That's all it takes!** What are you waiting for? **Stop and say a prayer right now!**

Did you say a prayer and accept God's gift of forgiveness? ❏

If you answered "yes," congratulations! You are a Christian! Oh yeah, and it means you are a winner in the only race that matters. If you did not understand some of the verses above and you aren't quite sure you are ready to accept God's gift of forgiveness, please talk to someone who can help you understand what it means to be a Christian. Maybe it's your pastor, parents, or a relative. Maybe it's your friend's mom. Find someone who knows what it means to be a Christian and tell them you want to know more! **Now, pump that fist in the air and take your victory lap, you champion, you!** *

PLAYBILL

GET TO KNOW YOUR
FAVORITE BIBLE CHARACTERS

by Susan Jones

Name: Jonah

Occupation: Prophet
(someone who tells people
about God's Word and delivers
messages straight from God)

Hometown: Gath Hepher

Life Story: Jonah's life is a
lesson for all of us!

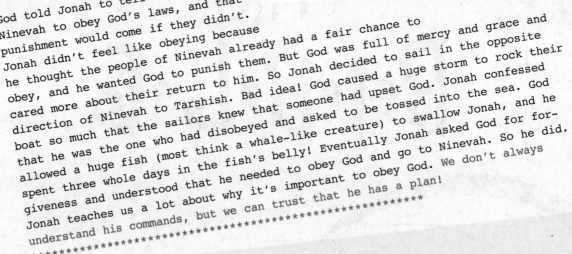

God told Jonah to tell the people of Ninevah to obey God's laws, and that punishment would come if they didn't. Jonah didn't feel like obeying because he thought the people of Ninevah already had a fair chance to obey, and he wanted God to punish them. But God was full of mercy and grace and cared more about their return to him. So Jonah decided to sail in the opposite direction of Ninevah to Tarshish. Bad idea! God caused a huge storm to rock their boat so much that the sailors knew that someone had upset God. Jonah confessed that he was the one who had disobeyed and asked to be tossed into the sea. God allowed a huge fish (most think a whale-like creature) to swallow Jonah, and he spent three whole days in the fish's belly! Eventually Jonah asked God for forgiveness and understood that he needed to obey God and go to Ninevah. So he did. Jonah teaches us a lot about why it's important to obey God. We don't always understand his commands, but we can trust that he has a plan!
****

Name: Noah

Occupation: Ark Builder Extraordinaire

Hometown: Exact whereabouts unknown

Life Story: Noah was a man who followed God.

Many years after creating man (Noah was around 600 years old!), God became saddened about the wickedness that had overtaken everyone. So God decided to send a flood to destroy almost all the earth. In his grace, however, he told Noah to build an ark and fill it with his family and animals so that they could repopulate the earth. Even though it sounded crazy, Noah obeyed, and sure enough, he and his family were saved when God sent the flood. After the flood God provided a rainbow in the sky as a promise to all mankind that he would never flood the earth again. Whew!
****

Name: **Joseph**
Occupation: **Sheep-herder,**
Dream Interpreter
Hometown: **Canaan**
Life Story: **Joseph had a full life!**

He was born into a big family of eleven brothers and one sister. Joseph's dad really liked him and gave him a coat of many colors. That made his brothers very jealous. To make matters worse, Joseph had dreams that his brothers would one day bow down to him and told his brothers about them. You might imagine how well that went over. Yep, it got Joseph into some trouble—but God had plans! His brothers didn't exactly like the idea of bowing down to Joseph, nor the fact that he was the "favorite son" so they sold him to some Egyptian travelers to be their slave! While Joseph was in Egypt, he had some ups and down, but eventually God elevated him from a slave to one of Pharaoh's favorites! God gave Joseph the ability to interpret dreams, so Pharaoh liked him a lot. He put Joseph in charge of the whole land. After many years famine overtook Canaan, where Joseph's brothers lived. Hearing Egypt had food, the brothers left Canaan and traveled to Egypt. When they arrived, God had prepared Joseph to be gracious to his brothers and forgive them. Joseph allowed them to have food and didn't hold a grudge against them for selling him into slavery so many years ago. He even said, "You intended to harm me, but God intended it for good to accomplish what is now being done, the saving of many lives." Joseph's story teaches us that sometimes when bad things happen, God has a bigger plan that is for good! He also teaches us to forgive those who harm us (like "mean girls" at school).
****

Name: Ruth

Occupation: Homemaker, Maidservant

Hometown: Moab, then Bethlehem

Life Story: Ruth was a Moabitess, a particular group of people who did not follow God.

Her husband died and left her with his mother, Naomi. Ruth wasn't sure what to do, and Naomi urged her to stay in Moab. But Ruth insisted that she go with Naomi to Bethlehem. Ruth said, "Where you go, I will go, and where you stay, I will stay. Your people will be my people, and your God, my God." She joined Naomi on her return to Bethlehem (a sign that Ruth now also followed God). There she met an amazing guy named Boaz (bow-as). God took care of her and allowed her to marry Boaz and have a son named Obed. Obed had a son named Jesse, and then Jesse had a son named David! So Ruth is the great-grandmother to David!
****

Name: David

Occupation: Shepherd, Sling-master, Poet, King

Hometown: Bethlehem, Gibeah, Hebron, Jerusalem

Life Story: David grew up as the youngest of Jesse's eight sons.

As a youth, David was a shepherd until God told the prophet Samuel that David would be the next king. David made some people notice him when he killed the giant, Goliath, with a mere slingshot! Sadly, when Samuel told people that David would be king, Saul, the current king, wasn't very happy about it. David spent a lot of time running away from King Saul, who was trying to kill him. Through that experience David learned God will take care of our enemies, and we are not to take matters into our own hands. Once David became king, he enjoyed much triumph and followed God (with a few missteps). He is described in the Bible as a "man after God's heart." He wrote a lot of the book of Psalms, but perhaps his greatest legacy is being on Jesus' family tree (check out Romans 1:3).
****

Name: **Daniel**

Occupation: **Prophet, Advisor to Rulers**

Hometown: **Jerusalem, then Babylon**

Life Story: **As a child, Daniel was taken from his hometown of Jerusalem to a place called Babylon.**

Daniel was an Israelite, one of God's special people, and different kings were taking Israelites captive and shipping them off to their lands. Throughout his entire captivity, Daniel served God faithfully. He refused to eat food that God told him not to, and God rewarded him by making him stronger than any of the king's men. Then God gave Daniel the ability to interpret dreams, so the king grew to like Daniel. Daniel's friends, Shadrach, Meshach, and Abednego, were also faithful to God and refused to worship any other thing aside from God. Remember the fiery furnace story? God spared their lives, just as he spared Daniel later when another king was tricked into throwing Daniel into a den of lions for continuing to pray to God, disobeying the king's command. God delivered many messages to Daniel, and he even had a special encounter with an angel! Daniel was a faithful prophet, committed to obeying God above all else, even if it meant facing lions!

****

Name: **Esther**

Occupation: **Queen**

Hometown: **Persia**

Life Story: **As a child, Esther's parents died, and her cousin, Mordecai, adopted her.**

She was brought to the king's palace to participate in a beauty ritual for twelve months (the ultimate spa package), after which the king picked a new queen. Esther was chosen and became the queen. Unfortunately she encountered some mean guys, like Haman, who wanted to kill Jews. Esther was a Jew, and she couldn't keep quiet for too long. After a few tries, she summoned the courage to ask the king to spare the Jews from the destruction Haman had planned. The king agreed and Esther's courage and strength in God saved lives. Esther's life is a great lesson in believing God puts us in certain places for his purposes. As Mordecai told Esther, "Who knows? Perhaps you have come to the kingdom for such a time as this."

****

Name that Character!

Using the characters on the last four pages, guess who is described below. Then, use the letters in the boxes to find out what Bible character is known for having a king for a dad, and a best friend who took the job after his dad! Hint: his BF is the guy on page 90!

Known for disobeying God, and going the wrong direction

☐ _ _ _ _ _

Known for his colorful attire and faith in God

☐ _ _ _ _ _

Known for great courage and strength to defend God—even if it did mean risking his life

_ _ ☐ _ _ _

Known for having faith in God and being a great warrior

_ _ _ ☐ _ _ _

Known for following God and marrying a super guy

☐ _ _ _

Known for risking her life for Israel.

_ _ ☐ _ _ _

Known for killing a giant, tending sheep and being a great king

☐ _ _ _ _

Known for obeying God's command to build a pretty big boat

☐ _ _ _

(Answers in order: Jonah, Joseph, Daniel, Joshua, Esther, Ruth, David, Noah.)

Name: **Joshua**

Occupation: **Military commander, Spy**

Hometown: **Ephraim**

Life Story: **Joshua was one of the Israelites hanging out with Moses in the desert.**

Moses sent him and eleven other spies on a special assignment to check out the land of Canaan (the land that God promised to the Israelites). When they returned, most of the spies told Moses that the land was great, but the people in the land were too scary to conquer. Joshua and Caleb were the only ones who had faith that God would allow them to win the battle for the land that he had promised! Once Moses died (at 120 years old!), God filled Joshua with wisdom and spoke to him. He told Joshua to lead the Israelites and prepare them to cross the Jordan River over to the promised land. So he did. And Joshua became known for many victories because of the Lord's provision. You may have heard of his first big win: Jericho. God really showed off by having Joshua march his troops around the city seven times, causing the city's wall to collapse. Joshua teaches us about having faith in God, despite scary circumstances and the fear of other people.
****

Super-Chick Cooking 101

Sensational Student S'mores

You will need:

4 oz. hard work squares

1 package teachable crackers

1 bag stick-to-it-puffs

1 fire of enthusiasm

1 extra-long study stick

1 set promptness gloves

Find a durable **study** stick and sharpen until you get it just right. If needed, **ask for help,** which is an excellent teachable quality. Get a fire of **enthusiasm** going until good and hot. Melt 4 oz. of **hard work** squares and spread onto **teachable** crackers. Place puffs on end of stick and roast over fire. **Don't give up** until the stick-to-it-puffs are done well. Use **promptness** gloves in assembling together with crackers and squares, and serve up to teachers. Be forewarned . . . teachers love these treats so much they always want s'more!

Beauty
by the
Book
the Good Book, that is!

by vicki courtney

Have you ever seen all the beauty tips listed on the magazine covers in the supermarket checkout line? Three easy steps to a zit-free complexion! Eye shadows that make your eyes pop! Six weeks to six pack abs! Fall fashions that will have the guys falling for you! 100 jeans that scream "nice butt!"

I promise I didn't make that last one up—I saw it on a magazine cover! Think about how stupid that is . . . have you ever had a pair of jeans that has screamed anything? Not to mention, if they scream words like that, they need to go to time-out.

What does God have to say about all these beauty tips? Believe it or not, he does have an opinion on the matter. Look at what the Bible has to say:

> I praise you because I am fearfully and wonderfully made; your works are wonderful, I know that full well.
> —Psalm 139:14 (NIV)

What it means:

You are created in the image of God and God doesn't make junk! Every person is unique and different, like a snowflake. No two are the same. God sees you as a masterpiece and when you look in the mirror, he wants you to "know that full well." Try this beauty tip: Every morning when you look in the mirror, say Psalm 139:14 and smile. You might even tape the verse up on your mirror as a reminder!

> But the Lord said to Samuel, "Do not consider his appearance or his height, for I have rejected him. The Lord does not look at the things man looks at. Man looks at the outward appearance, but the Lord looks at the heart."
> —1 Samuel 16:7 (NIV)

What it means:

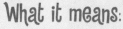

The world focuses on what people look like on the outside. God focuses on what people look like on the inside. Do you put more time and effort into being pretty on the outside or the inside? As you get older, you will meet Christian girls who spend more time trying to find the perfect outfit, get the perfect tan, find the perfect lip gloss, and have the perfect body. While there's nothing wrong with wanting to look pretty, we need to make sure it's in balance. God would rather see us work on becoming drop-dead gorgeous on the inside. You know, the kind of girl who talks to him on a regular basis (prayer) and reads her Bible. (See page 79 for tips on revving up your prayer life.)

Charm is deceptive, and beauty is fleeting; but a woman who fears the LORD is to be praised.

–Proverbs 31:30 (NIV)

What it means:

Beauty fades with age, so if you are more concerned with your outer appearance, you will be unhappy when the wrinkles come and the number on the scale goes up. In fact, did you know that your body may show the beginning signs of aging as early as age twenty? I know that may seem old to you, but that's not very old! You may notice fine wrinkles begin to appear, thinning skin, lack of firmness in your hands and neck, graying hair, hair loss, and thinning nails.[1] Ugh! I guess the Bible is right when it says, "Beauty fades with age!"

That is why God wants us to "fear" him. That doesn't mean to be afraid of him, but rather to be in awe of him and all he has done. Let me put it to you this way. If you stand two girls next to each other and one is Miss Teen USA and the other is a more average looking girl who loves the Lord more than anything, she is the more beautiful girl in the eyes of God.

Your beauty should not come from outward adornment, such as braided hair and the wearing of gold jewelry and fine clothes. Instead, it should be that of your inner self, the unfading beauty of a gentle and quiet spirit, which is of great worth in God's sight.
–1 Peter 3:3-4 (NIV)

What it means:

This does not mean it's wrong to braid your hair or wear nice clothes and jewelry. The verse was written to warn women not to follow the customs of some of the Egyptian women who, during that time period, spent hours and hours working on their hair, make-up, and finding the perfect outfit. God would rather see women work on becoming beautiful on the inside— the kind of beauty that lasts forever.

Physical training is good, but training for godliness is much better, promising benefits in this life and in the life to come.
–1 Timothy 4:8 (NLT)

What it means:

Exercising and staying in shape is a good thing, but God expects us to stay in shape spiritually by reading our Bibles, praying, and going to church on a regular basis. In other words, there will be plenty of people who put their time and effort into staying in shape but are out of shape, spiritually. If they don't know Jesus Christ, their perfect bodies won't get them through the gates of heaven.

1. See www.cnn.com/2007/HEALTH/07/27/life.stages/index.html.

Dig into God's Word!

by Susan Jones

Have you ever been to a museum and seen fossils? Maybe you've seen one of a dinosaur, insect, or fish. It always amazes me that scientists take months, and sometimes even years, to carefully dig through tons and tons of dirt just to find the skeleton of something that lived and died a very long time ago. But, to them, excavating that skeleton was important, crucial even, to their jobs. They valued the information that the skeleton would give them and gladly did the work to get to their "treasure," the fossil.

Sometimes studying the Bible is the same way. To really get to the treasure, we must first do some digging. Reading and understanding the Bible isn't always easy, but the reward is well worth the work!

THE TOOLS

Before we can begin digging, we need to understand the tools we'll be using.

1. Bible

Layout: The Bible is divided into two sections, the Old Testament and New Testament. The entire Bible is God's inspired work, so it is all important, and it has the same message of redemption from beginning to end.

The Old Testament takes place from creation to a time prior to Jesus' birth. The Old and New Testaments have about a 400-year gap between them. The New Testament picks up with Jesus being born. Revelation ends the New Testament with the prophecy, or future-telling, of the end of times here on Earth as well as a glimpse of what we can expect afterward in heaven.

In the New Testament, if your Bible has red words, it means that Jesus said them.

Table of Contents: Sometimes it can be hard to find a particular book. So each Bible has a list in the first few pages to tell you the order, and even a starting page number for each of the 66 books. From there, you'd look for the chapter and verse. When you see a passage listed like this, John 3:16, it is referencing the book of John, the third chapter, sixteenth verse.

Concordance: Most Bibles include a listing near the back where you can find verses that include a particular word. Let's say you wanted to look up a verse about being afraid. If you looked up *afraid*, you'd find Psalm 56:3, "When I am afraid, I will trust in you."

Most Bibles also include cross-references or footnotes. These are teeny little letters you sometimes see slightly above a word in a verse. It looks like this [a]. If this appears over a word, it is telling you that either this word appears in other similar verses or it is telling you a note about that particular word or verse. The cross-references are usually listed in the middle column on the page or at the very bottom. You would look at the chapter and verse you were reading, then find the matching letter in the notes section. If it is a cross-reference, it would list other verses that include the referenced word. If it is a footnote (usually at the bottom of the page), it will tell you something about that word.

2. Journal

While a journal is not absolutely necessary, it can be a very helpful tool to write out the things that God teaches you.

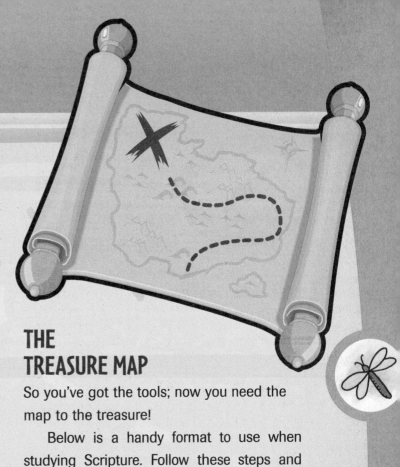

THE TREASURE MAP

So you've got the tools; now you need the map to the treasure!

Below is a handy format to use when studying Scripture. Follow these steps and begin digging.

See

First thing's first. Read it and let it sink in a little. Don't read too much at a time so you can focus. Look for words that are repeated, words that are strong or action-oriented, words that stand out, and words such as "therefore" and "so" (they indicate cause and effect relationships).

Think

Think about what the verses are trying to communicate. Ask yourself these questions:

What do these verses mean?

What is the theme?

Is it asking me to do something?

Look for patterns that compare things, such as "the wise man does X, but the foolish man does Y" and make a chart with lists underneath each category.

If you have a hard time understanding what certain verses mean, do not be shy about asking Mom, Dad, or a church teacher about it. Another idea is to use a Bible written in a translation that is easier to understand.

Feel

After reading and thinking about the meaning of these verses, how does it affect my feelings toward God, myself, and others? Does it reveal a sin that I should feel sorry about? Does it make me love God more because I have learned about him? For example, reading John 3:16 might make you feel grateful to God for sending Jesus to save us.

Do

Time for action! How does this verse affect my behavior or thoughts? Does it show me how to think or act differently than I already am? What can I do to apply this verse to my life?

IT'S TIME TO DIG!

Reference the "treasure map" to help you excavate God's truth by looking at James 1:19–20. Write out some thoughts to these questions to help you.

1. See: What words jump out to me?

2. Think: What do these verses mean?

3. Feel: How do these verses make me feel about God, myself, or others?

4. Do: What am I going to do in my life now because of these verses?

Finish by praying. It's always important to pray while you are reading and studying the Bible. Ask God to show you the treasure that he wants you to have from reading his word. Happy digging!

Where to DIG

Here are some Bible reading plans to give you an idea of where to start digging into God's word on a regular basis. Also, check out "Favorite Bible Verses" on page 114.

* Proverb a day for a month

Read one chapter a day from Proverbs for one month. Since Proverbs has 31 chapters, you can read the entire book of Proverbs in one month.

* Psalm a day for a year

Read one chapter a day from Psalms for the entire year and you will read through the book of Psalms twice.

* Psalm and a proverb a day for five months

Read one chapter from the book of Psalms and one chapter from the book of Proverbs a day for five months and you will read through the book of Psalms once and book of Proverbs five times.

* Five verses a day

Read five verses a day from anywhere in the Bible. (Look below at the New Testament book-a-month section for a great place to start).

* Topical

Look up verses in your concordance about a particular topic, and study a different topic each week.

FOR THE DEEP-DIGGERS

* One New Testament chapter a day for a year
* Read one chapter a day from the New Testament five days a week. This will allow you to read through the entire New Testament in a year (260 chapters).

* New Testament book a month

Choose a shorter New Testament book to read every week (usually about one chapter a day) for the entire month. By the end of the month, you will have read through the book four times (which helps to remember it!).

Some suggestions: January: James; February: Philippians; March: 1 John; April: 1 Peter; May: 2 Peter; June: 1 Timothy; July: Ephesians; August: Galatians; September: Colossians; October: 1 Thessalonians; November: Titus; December: 2 Timothy.

Quiz

That's Wild!

by Susan Jones

Take this quiz to learn about animals in the Bible.

1. How many of each animal did Noah take into the ark?

(A) two
(B) three
(C) seven

2. When God created everything, on what day did he create animals?

(A) second and third
(B) seventh and eighth
(C) fifth and sixth

3. When Moses got the Ten Commandments on Mount Sinai from God, he came down the mountain to find the Israelites worshipping a golden statue of what creature?

(A) a zebra
(B) a calf
(C) a dog

4. When Daniel refused to worship anyone but God, he was thrown into a den of what?

(A) hamsters
(B) lions
(C) alligators

5. In an effort to display his power to Pharaoh, God told Moses and Aaron to throw down Aaron's rod, and it would be turned into what?

(A) a snake
(B) a bird
(C) a frog

Answers:

1. **Both A and C are correct!—two AND seven** God told Noah to take seven pairs of each kind of clean animal and two of each kind of other animals (Genesis 6:19–20; 7:2–3). By "clean" the Bible means animals that were acceptable for sacrifice. Seven of the clean animals were taken so they could be sacrificed after the flood was over. If there were only two of an animal, a male and a female, and one was sacrificed, that species of animal would no longer exist. (www.gotquestions.org/Noahs-ark-questions.html)

2. **C-fifth and sixth**
Here's what God created on each day:
One: *light, day, night*
Two: *waters, sky*
Three: *land (Earth), plants, fruit trees, vegetation*
Four: *sun, moon, stars*
Five: *water animals and birds*
Six: *Land animals*

Genesis 1:24–31 tells us that God created all living creatures from livestock to "creatures that move along the ground, and wild animals" (NIV) on the sixth day. He even made man that very day!

3. **B-a calf** In the days of Moses, it was not uncommon to find people worshipping animals of all sorts. In this case, the Israelites, who knew better, decided to worship something they could see: a calf made out of gold. This angered Moses (and God) so much that he smashed the tablets of stone that contained the Ten Commandments! (Exodus 32). He had to go back up the mountain later to get another set from God (Exodus 34). (Note to self: Don't anger Moses, or God for that matter!)

4. **B-lions** Daniel was a great guy who loved God more than anything. He was living in a country where King Darius was ruler. Darius didn't know God, and his staff asked him to sign a document stating that all the people in the country had to worship him (Darius) alone for thirty days. Almost everyone obeyed, except Daniel. He believed that God was the only one to be worshipped, and he prayed three times a day to the one true God.

Darius really liked Daniel, but he felt he should enforce the law he put into place, so Darius had Daniel thrown into a den, or pit, with hungry lions (not like sweet Simba or Ayslan). The coolest part of this story is that Daniel lived! God protected him, and because of his faith, God used the situation to teach Darius a thing or two about how powerful he was. (P.S. Scholars believe Daniel was in his 80s when he was thrown into the den!)

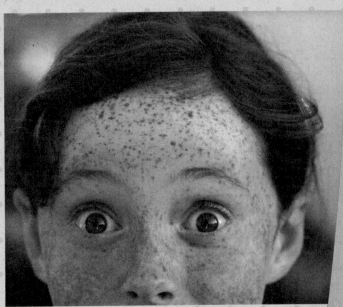

5. **A-a snake** Moses and his brother, Aaron, were stuck in Egypt as slaves with all the Israelites. God told Moses that he was going to lead them out of Egypt, and that Aaron would be the spokesperson for Moses.

So God told Moses to go to Pharaoh, the leader of Egypt, and have Aaron ask for permission for all Israelites to leave the country so they could worship God. God also told them to perform a miracle in front of Pharaoh to show off God's power.

So Aaron obeyed and he took his staff (similar to a long, straight cane) and threw it down on the ground. Sure enough, it turned into a snake! Here's the juicy part! Pharaoh wasn't really impressed, so he called in his own leaders to throw down their staffs, and they all turned into snakes too! When they did, Aaron's staff-snake ate up all the others (see Exodus 7:1–13). God—1; Pharaoh—None

Did you know? God uses snakes to teach the Israelites a lesson about God's power too! It happens after they've escaped Egypt and begin to complain about the food he provided for them. Check it out by reading Numbers 21:4–8.

YOU'VE GOT MAIL!!

by Julie Ferwerda

✔ God's Letters Reveal Radical Kid Stories

It's a known fact that Jesus loved kids—and personally, I think that's why he included so many of them in the Bible! Read the Scripture provided to come up with the name (or description) of the famous Bible kid below.

1. _____ He killed both bears and lions with basically his bare hands for trying to steal his sheep.
(1 Samuel 17:34–35)

2. _____ After dying from a super bad headache, this boy sneezed seven times and woke up when a cool prophet dude brought him back to life.
(2 Kings 4:32–36)

3. _____ He brought his sack lunch to a picnic and ended up sharing it with the whole town. (John 6:9—13)

4. _____ She was raised by her cousin after her parents died, and then ended up in a palace—probably the first ever orphan Queen. (Esther 2:7)

5. _____ This kid's long hair made him grow up big time buff for helping God get rid of bad, bad Philistines. As long as he grew the "do," he was unstoppably strong. (Judges 13:3—5)

6. _____ His parents waited one hundred years for this only son, and then God asked his dad to sacrifice him. At the last minute, God rescued him and then used his story to foretell people about the future sacrifice of his only Son (Jesus) thousands of years later. (Genesis 22:1—14)

7. _____ His dad (a jealous king) was trying to kill his best friend, but he was loyal to God by being loyal to his friend. (1 Samuel 23:14—18)

8. _____ She helped one of Pharaoh's daughters find a nursemaid for her little brother (his real mom) and later she became a prophetess. (Exodus 2:1—4; 15:20)

9. _____ He became the king of Israel at the age of eight and totally obeyed God, even though his own dad had been an evil king. (2 Kings 22:1—2)

10. _____ While being raised in the temple by a priest (his mom gave him to the Lord's service), a voice called his name four times in the night to give him a special message, but he didn't realize it was God speaking to him. (1 Samuel 3:1—10)

11. _____ She was visited by an angel who said, "You have found favor with God," and he gave her an ultra-important assignment that would change the world forever. (Luke 1:26—33)

12. _____ Feeling too young for the job when God gave him his life assignment, he's called "the weeping prophet," because of his sadness over people's sins. (Jeremiah 1:4—9)

13. _____ He got left behind by his parents at church when he was twelve but he was no doubt doing God's work. (Luke 2:41—47)

14. _____ She was chosen to take care of a famous and godly king in his last days on earth. (1 Kings 1:1—4)

15. _____ This baby and important future leader might have been crocodile food if he hadn't been discovered floating down a river in a basket and rescued. (Exodus 2:5—10)

Answers: 1–David; 2–The Shunammite's son; 3–Boy with 5 loaves and 2 fish; 4–Esther; 5–Samson; 6–Isaac; 7–Jonathan; 8–Miriam; 9–Josiah; 10–Samuel; 11–Mary; 12–Jeremiah; 13–Jesus; 14–Abishag; 15–Moses.

10

SUPER COOL THINGS *about:*

the Bible

by Julie Ferwerda

1. It was written by about 40 different God-inspired people more than 1,600 years ago.

2. It was the first-ever major printed and distributed book (printed in 1450).

3. It tells one main story from Genesis to Revelation: God sent his Son to save people from their sins and to give them eternal life.

4. It is the all-time best-selling book in history.

5. It's been translated into more languages than any other book (1,200).

6. It tells people the truth about where they came from and where they're going.

7. There is no conflict between the Bible and the true facts of science.

8. You can read it out loud in seventy hours.

9. The word *God* or *Lord* never appears in the book of Esther.

10. The Bible contains about 773,600 words!

A Word About the Future

by GOD

Jeremiah 6:16

This is what the LORD says: "Stand at the crossroads and look; ask for the ancient paths, ask where the good way is, and walk in it, and you will find rest for your souls.

Jeremiah 29:11

"For I know the plans I have for you," declares the LORD, "plans to prosper you and not to harm you, plans to give you hope and a future."

Psalm 25:4—5

Show me your ways, O LORD,
teach me your paths;
guide me in your truth and teach me,
for you are God my Savior,
and my hope is in you all day long.

Proverbs 3:5—6

Trust in the LORD with all your heart and lean not on your own understanding; in all your ways acknowledge him, and he will make your paths straight.

Proverbs 24:14

Know also that wisdom is sweet to your soul; if you find it, there is a future hope for you, and your hope will not be cut off.

Matthew 6:33 (KJV)

But seek ye first the kingdom of God, and his righteousness; and all these things shall be added unto you.

Ecclesiastes 7:14

When times are good, be happy; but when times are bad, consider: God has made the one as well as the other. Therefore, a man cannot discover anything about his future.

Ecclesiastes 8:7

Since no man knows the future, who can tell him what is to come?

Matthew 6:25—27

"Therefore I tell you, do not worry about your life, what you will eat or drink; or about your body, what you will wear. Is not life more important than food, and the body more important than clothes? Look at the birds of the air; they do not sow or reap or store away in barns, and yet your heavenly Father feeds them. Are you not much more valuable than they? Who of you by worrying can add a single hour to his life?

Matthew 28:19—20

Therefore go and make disciples of all nations, baptizing them in the name of the Father and of the Son and of the Holy Spirit, and teaching them to obey everything I have commanded you. And surely I am with you always, to the very end.

Quiz

aRe you KiddinG Me?

by Susie Davis

There are lots of super silly sounding stories in the Bible. And some are so strange you might hear them and say, "Are you kidding me?!" Take the quiz below to see if you know the correct answers to some of the weirder facts in the Bible.

1. In the Old Testament, Joshua was in charge of making sure all the Israelites got a fair share of land after wandering in the wildness for forty years. He based his decision on who got what piece of land by . . .

A) reading palms.
B) rolling dice.
C) testing the wind.

2. In the Old Testament, King Saul often tried to chase down and kill David who was chosen by God to become king. In an effort to escape Saul and find safety, David . . .

A) scratched on doors and slobbered like a crazy man.

B) issued a vote in Israel to see who was more popular.

C) dressed up like a girl so that Saul wouldn't recognize him.

3. Moses went up Mount Sinai on special assignment to get God's Commandments. How many Commandments did God end up carving on the stone tablets?

A) 10

B) 20

C) 50

4. Isaiah was a prophet in the Old Testament. God asked Isaiah to . . .

A) gather flowers, pull off the petals and say out loud to the Israelites, "He loves you. He loves you not."

B) become king at the age of fifteen and rule the people with wisdom.

C) run around naked and barefoot.

5. King Herod, in the New Testament, died of . . .

A) old age.

B) a bad case of stomach worms.

C) a sword wound to his heart.

6. Ezekiel, an Old Testament prophet, was commanded by God to . . .

A) preach a sermon in sign language.

B) preach a sermon to the birds of the air and the flowers in the field.

C) preach a sermon to a valley of dry bones

Answers:

1. **The correct answer is B.** Though it might not seem very spiritual to roll dice for a piece of land, that is exactly what Joshua did. In the book of Joshua, you can read about how Joshua "cast sacred lots" in the presence of God. A "lot" was probably a small stone-like object that was thrown or "cast" on the ground. The way it fell to the ground determined the answer to the question. Check out Joshua 18:3–6 that describes the scene, "Then Joshua asked them, 'How long are

you going to wait before taking possession of the remaining land the LORD, the God of your ancestors, has given to you? Select three men from each tribe, and I will send them out to explore the land and map it out. They will then return to me with a written report of their proposed divisions of their new home-land. Let them divide the land into seven sections, excluding Judah's territory in the south and Joseph's territory in the north. And when you record the seven divisions of the land and bring them to me, I will cast sacred lots in the presence of the LORD our God to assign land to each tribe'" (NLT). Now, while casting lots seems a lot like what we do now when we draw straws or flip a coin, it was reserved for big decisions that needed major direction. And you will note that Joshua said that he would cast "sacred lots in the presence of the Lord our God," which sounds a little more serious than flipping a quarter to see which team gets the kick off!

2. Crazy as it seems, the correct answer is A.

In order to find safety, David acted like he was insane! David was trying to find a place to live away from Saul so he headed over to Gath but when he arrived, there was just more trouble awaiting him. We find the story in 1 Samuel 21:10–15, "So David escaped from Saul and went to King Achish of Gath. But the officers of Achish were unhappy about his being there. "Isn't this David, the king of the land?" they asked. "Isn't he the one the people honor with dances, singing, 'Saul has killed his thousands, and David his ten thousands'?" David heard these comments and was very afraid of what King Achish of Gath might do to him. So he pretended to be insane, scratching on doors and drooling down his beard. Finally, King Achish said to his men, "Must you bring me a madman? We already have enough of them around here! Why should I let someone like this be my guest?" Though David must have been very frightened, you have to admit that he did some pretty quick thinking and pulled off a very believable act. Guess he was a really good actor!

3. The correct answer is B. God only gave us ten Commandments but he had to inscribe them twice because Moses got really angry. See, the Israelites were worshiping a golden calf (not a good thing to do) and Moses got so mad at them that he threw down the first copy, smashing it into pieces. In Exodus 32 Moses met God at Mount Sinai and inscribed the first set on stone tablets. Then Moses had a fit and destroyed them. Then in Exodus 34, Moses met God at Mount Sinai again and inscribed the second set on stone tablets. So in all, though God gave us ten Commandments, he inscribed them twice.

4. The correct answer is C. God had the prophet Isaiah wander around naked to make a point. He wanted Isaiah to act out the defeat of Egypt and Ethiopia. I know it sounds a little extreme but check it out yourself. Isaiah 20:1–6 says, "King Sargon

of Assyria gave orders for his army commander to capture the city of Ashdod. About this same time the LORD had told me, "Isaiah, take off everything, including your sandals!" I did this and went around naked and barefoot for three years. Then the LORD said: What Isaiah has done is a warning to Egypt and Ethiopia. Everyone in these two

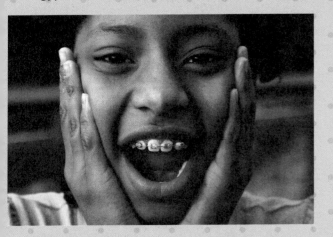

countries will be led away naked and barefoot by the king of Assyria. Young or old, they will be taken prisoner, and Egypt will be disgraced. They will be confused and frustrated, because they depended on Ethiopia and bragged about Egypt. When this happens, the people who live along the coast will say, "Look what happened to them! We ran to them for safety, hoping they would protect us from the king of Assyria. But now, there is no escape for us" (CEV). Whew . . . that was a tough job from God. It makes honoring your mother and father sound like a piece of cake!

5. The coRRect answeR is ReaLLy GRoss . . . it's B . . . a stomach full of worms! See, Herod got a little big for his britches from all the people's praise and his pride actually killed him. Don't believe me? It's all in Acts 12:22–23, "The people gave him a great ovation, shouting, 'It's the voice of a god, not of a man!' Instantly, an angel of the Lord struck Herod

with a sickness, because he accepted the people's worship instead of giving the glory to God. So he was consumed with worms and died" (NLT).

6. The coRRect answeR is C. Just another case of God asking a prophet to do something a tad unusual. Read God's instructions here in Ezekiel 37:1–6, "The LORD took hold of me, and I was carried away by the Spirit of the LORD to a valley filled with bones. He led me all around among the bones that covered the valley floor. They were scattered everywhere across the ground and were completely dried out. Then he asked me, 'Son of man, can these bones become living people again?' 'O Sovereign LORD,' I replied, 'you alone know the answer to that.' Then he said to me, 'Speak a prophetic message to these bones and say, Dry bones, listen to the word of the LORD! This is what the Sovereign LORD says: Look! I am going to put breath into you and make you live again! I will put flesh and muscles on you and cover you with skin. I will put breath into you, and you will come to life. Then you will know that I am the LORD'" (NLT). While that in itself is pretty strange, you gotta read further in Ezekiel 37 to see what God makes happen just because Ezekiel obeyed!

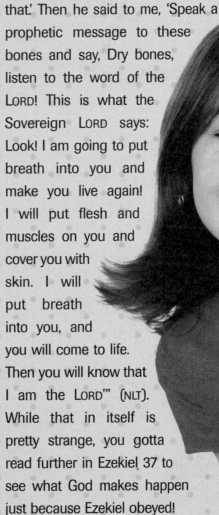

by Vicki Courtney

To Whom are You Listening?

When it comes to making money, the world says: "The more you make the happier you'll be." **The Word says:** *"It is easier for a camel to go through the eye of a needle than for a rich person to enter the Kingdom of God."* (Matthew 19:24)

When it comes to possessions, the world says: "He who has the most toys wins." **The Word says:** *"Don't store up treasures here on earth, where they can be eaten by moths and get rusty, and where thieves break in and steal. Store your treasures in heaven, where they will never become moth-eaten or rusty and where they will be safe from thieves."* (Matthew 6:19–20 NLT)

The Word says: "Don't copy the behavior and customs of this world, but let God transform you into a new person by changing the way you think."

When it comes to dressing immodest, the world says: "If you've got it, flaunt it!" **The Word says:** *"And I want women to be modest in their appearance. They should wear decent and appropriate clothing and not draw attention to themselves."* (1 Timothy 2:9 NLT)

When it comes to following the crowd and peer pressure, the world says: "You have to do it if you want to fit in!" **The Word says:** *"Don't copy the behavior and customs of this world, but let God transform you into a new person by changing the way you think. Then you will know what God wants you to do, and you will know how good and pleasing and perfect his will really is."* (Romans 12:2 NLT)

When it comes to feeling good about yourself, the world says: "Worth equals what you look like."

The Word says:
"Man does not see what the Lord sees, for man sees what is visible, but the Lord sees the heart."
(1 Samuel 16:7)

The Word says:
"I am the way and the truth and the life and no one comes to the Father except through Me."

When it comes to saying bad words, the world says:
"Everybody talks that way!"
The Word says: *"Obscene stories, foolish talk, and coarse jokes—these are not for you. Instead, let there be thankfulness to God."* (Ephesians 5:4 NLT)

When it comes to sharing about your faith in Jesus,
the world says: "Don't do it! You might offend someone!"
The Word says: *"Go out and train everyone you meet, far and near, in this way of life, marking them by baptism in the threefold name: Father, Son, and Holy Spirit."* (Matthew 28:19 *The Message*)

When it comes to illegally downloading music,
the world says: "Who cares? Everyone does it!"
The Word says: *"You must not steal."*
(Leviticus 19:11; Romans 13:9)

When it comes to heaven, the world says:
"No worries! As long as you're a good person, you're in!"
The Word says: *"You can enter God's Kingdom only through the narrow gate. The highway to hell is broad, and its gate is wide for the many who choose the easy way. But the gateway to life is small, and the road is narrow, and only a few ever find it."*
(Matthew 7:13–14 NLT)

When it comes to other faiths, the world says:
"Many paths lead to the same God."
The Word says: *"I am the way and the truth and the life. No one comes to the Father except through me."* (John 14:6 NIV)

What's Your Favorite Bible Verse?

by Vicki Courtney

When I was ten years old, my grandparents gave me a Bible for Christmas. I had never owned a Bible before, but I somehow knew that it was no ordinary book. I remember climbing up on my bed and flipping through the crisp pages. In the front of the Bible was the 23rd Psalm and so I figured that it must be important. I remember trying to memorize the Psalm and I can still say it to this day. I guess that would have to be my first official favorite Bible passage. Today I have many favorite verses and passages from the Bible, and it would be impossible to list them all. I read the Bible just about every day and it never grows old to me.

When we surveyed girls your age and asked them what their favorite Bible verse/passage was, we got many different answers. I was so impressed with how many of you have already fallen in love with God's Word! Below, you will find some of the verses/passages girls shared. Is your favorite on the list?

First Place goes to:

"For God so loved the world that he gave his one and only Son, that whoever believes in him shall not perish but have eternal life." —John 3:16 (NIV)

Ashley, 9; Anne, 11; Tate, 10; Kaleigh, 10; Kayla, 10; Danielle, 11; Kristin, 12; Lauren, 11; Casie, 10; Lauren, 10; Valerie, 9; Jessica, 8; Jaimee, 10; Olivia, 9; Stephanie, 9; Gia, 9; Ellie, 9; Morgan, 10; Elise, 10; Melissa, 9; Riley, 10; Melissa, 11; Ashton, 10; Hope, 8; Sydney, 10; Emily, 12; Sarah, 8½; Saige, 10; Allison, 8½; Madeline, 10; Angela, 8; Kennan, 8; Amber, 9; Gabi, 12; Alex, 11; Angela, 12; Morgan, 11; Brittany, 10; Meagan, 10; Karon, 11; Emma, 9; Danielle, 9; Addison, 11; Ellie, 11; Bailey, 10; Heather, 9½; Mollie, 12

"They cried to you and were saved; in you they trusted and were not disappointed." —Psalm 22:5 (NIV)
Rachel, 10; Emily, 10

"For I know the plans I have for you," declares the LORD, "plans to prosper you and not to harm you, plans to give you hope and a future." —Jeremiah 29:11
Helen, 12

"I will lie down and sleep in peace, for you alone, O LORD, make me dwell in safety." —Psalm 4:8
Theresa, 12

"You made him a little lower than the angels; you crowned him with glory and honor and put everything under his feet. In putting everything under him, God left nothing that is not subject to him. Yet at present we do not see everything subject to him. But we see Jesus, who was made a little lower than the angels, now crowned with glory and honor because he suffered death, so that by the grace of God he might taste death for everyone. In bringing many sons to glory, it was fitting that God, for whom and through whom everything exists, should make the author of their salvation perfect through suffering." —Hebrews 2:7—10 (NIV)
Savannah, 12

"I can do everything through him who gives me strength." —Philippians 4:13 (NIV)
Laura, 10; Mara, 10; April, 11; Corinne, 11; Kaelyn, 12

"But you will receive power when the Holy Spirit comes on you; and you will be my witnesses in Jerusalem, and in all Judea and Samaria, and to the ends of the earth." —Acts 1:8
Corrie, 11

The LORD is my shepherd, I shall not be in want. He makes me lie down in green pastures, he leads me beside quiet waters, he restores my soul. He guides me in paths of righteousness for his name's sake. Even though I walk through the valley of the shadow of death, I will fear no evil, for you are with me; your rod and your staff, they comfort me. You prepare a table before me in the presence of my enemies. You anoint my head with oil; my cup overflows. Surely goodness and love will follow me all the days of my life, and I will dwell in the house of the LORD forever. —Psalm 23 (NIV)
Kristie, 11; Zahara, 11

"Be shepherds of God's flock that is under your care, serving as overseers—not because you must, but because you are willing, as God wants you to be; not greedy for money, but eager to serve; not lording it over those entrusted to you, but being examples to the flock. And when the Chief Shepherd appears, you will receive the crown of glory that will never fade away." —1 Peter 5:2—4
Stephanie, 11

Hebrews 2:7-10

"For what I do is not the good I want to do; no, the evil I do not want to do—this I keep on doing." —Romans 7:19
Chloe, 9

May God be gracious to us and bless us and make his face shine upon us, that your ways may be known on earth, your salvation among all nations. May the peoples praise you, O God; may all the peoples praise you. May the nations be glad and sing for joy, for you rule the peoples justly and guide the nations of the earth. May the peoples praise you, O God; may all the peoples praise you. Then the land will yield its harvest, and God, our God, will bless us. God will bless us, and all the ends of the earth will fear him. —Psalm 67 (NIV)
Taylor, 11

"I have hidden your word in my heart that I might not sin against you." —Psalm 119:11
Julie, 11

"This made the Jews ask, "Will he kill himself? Is that why he says, 'Where I go, you cannot come'?" —John 8:22
Victoria, 8

"Have I not commanded you? Be strong and courageous. Do not be terrified; do not be discouraged, for the LORD your God will be with you wherever you go." –Joshua 1:9
Marissa, 10; Amy, 12

"For we are God's workmanship, created in Christ Jesus to do good works, which God prepared in advance for us to do." —Ephesians 2:10
Katie, 9½

"And we know that in all things God works for the good of those who love him, who have been called according to his purpose." —Romans 8:28
Elise, 12

"But the fruit of the Spirit is love, joy, peace, patience, kindness, goodness, faithfulness, gentleness and self-control. Against such things there is no law." —Galatians 5:22–23
Izzy, 8

"Finally, brothers, whatever is true, whatever is noble, whatever is right, whatever is pure, whatever is lovely, whatever is admirable—if anything is excellent or praiseworthy—think about such things." —Philippians 4:8
Bethany, 12

"Love the LORD your God with all your heart and with all your soul and with all your strength." —Deuteronomy 6:5
Jessica, 9

"Trust in the LORD with all your heart and lean not on your own understanding; in all your ways acknowledge him, and he will make your paths straight."
—Proverbs 3:5–6
Emma, 9½; Stephanie, 10½

"Jesus replied, 'They do not need to go away. You give them something to eat.'"
—Matthew 14:16
Keagan, 10

"Your word is a lamp to my feet and a light to my path." —Psalm 119:105
Danielle, 11

"Therefore go and make disciples of all nations, baptizing them in the name of the Father and of the Son and of the Holy Spirit, and teaching them to obey everything I have commanded you. And surely I am with you always, to the very end of the age." —Matthew 28: 19–20
Breanna, 12; Julia, 11

"For the LORD is good and his love endures forever; his faithfulness continues through all generations." —Psalm 100:5
Elizabeth, 10

"So do not fear, for I am with you; do not be dismayed, for I am your God. I will strengthen you and help you; I will uphold you with my righteous right hand." —Isaiah 41:10
Sarah, 10

"My heart is steadfast, O God; I will sing and make music with all my soul." —Psalm 108:1
Laney, 9

"I lift up my eyes to the hills— where does my help come from? My help comes from the LORD, the Maker of heaven and earth."
—Psalm 121:1–2
Samantha, 10

"He who plots evil will be known as a schemer."
—Proverbs 24:8
Molly, 11

"The Word became flesh and made his dwelling among us. We have seen his glory, the glory of the One and Only, who came from the Father, full of grace and truth"
—John 1:14
Lara, 11½

John 1:14

"But he was pierced for our transgressions, he was crushed for our iniquities; the punishment that brought us peace was upon him, and by his wounds we are healed."
—Isaiah 53:5
Morgan, 11

"For this very reason, make every effort to add to your faith goodness; and to goodness, knowledge; and to knowledge, self-control; and to self-control, perseverance; and to perseverance, godliness; and to godliness, brotherly kindness; and to brotherly kindness, love. For if you possess these qualities in increasing measure, they will keep you from being ineffective and unproductive in your knowledge of our Lord Jesus Christ."
—2 Peter 1:5—8
Gretchen, 11¾

"People will come from east and west and north and south, and will take their places at the feast in the kingdom of God."
—Luke 13:29
Andie, 12½

"Do not be anxious about anything, but in everything, by prayer and petition, with thanksgiving, present your requests to God. And the peace of God, which transcends all understanding, will guard your hearts and your minds in Christ Jesus."
—Philippians 4:6—7
Katie, 11; Brittani, 11

"And whatever you do, whether in word or deed, do it all in the name of the Lord Jesus, giving thanks to God the Father through him." —Colossians 3:17
Taylor, 11

"Keep your lives free from the love of money and be content with what you have, because God has said, 'Never will I leave you; never will I forsake you.'"—Hebrews 13:5
Faith, (no age)

"For all have sinned and fall short of the glory of God." —Romans 3:23

Jenica, 11; Breeann, 11

"For he will command his angels concerning you to guard you in all your ways." —Psalm 91:11

Caroline, 9

"I praise you because I am fearfully and wonderfully made; your works are wonderful, I know that full well." —Psalm 139:14

Kimberly, 11

"I am the way and the truth and the life. No one comes to the Father except through me." —John 14:6

Erin, 9; Judianne, 9

"But those who hope in the LORD will renew their strength. They will soar on wings like eagles; they will run and not grow weary, they will walk and not be faint." —Isaiah 40:31

Rachel, 11

"Don't let anyone look down on you because you are young, but set an example for the believers in speech, in life, in love, in faith and in purity." —1 Timothy 4:12

Rainie, 11

"Know that the LORD is God. It is he who made us, and we are his; we are his people, the sheep of his pasture." —Psalm 100:3

Zoe, 11

"A perverse man stirs up dissension, and a gossip separates close friends." —Proverbs 16:28

Raegan, 11

(For added meaning, visit "Dig into God's Word" on page 98 and use the study method provided on these passages!)

1 Timothy 4:12

Chapter 4:
Friends, Family, & Others

Follow the LEADER?

by Scout Courtney

Me & Lexie.

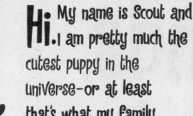

hatchin' some trouble

Hi. My name is Scout and I am pretty much the cutest puppy in the universe—or at least that's what my family tells me. I wanted to talk to you (yeah, dogs talk) about the dangers of following the leader. You see, I have a big sister, Lexie, who is also a Yorkshire Terrier just like me. Lexie is about four years older than me and she weighs about six pounds. Sometimes that makes me kinda mad because I only weigh three pounds and it's hard for me to keep up with her and jump on stuff like couches and chairs. When I was about five months old, I finally figured out how to jump on the couch just like Lexie. I don't think Lexie was real happy about me learning to jump on the couch because when I would follow her, she would

> I wanted to prove how cool I was, so I followed her.

jump up higher on the top of the back cushions to get away from me.

One day I wanted to prove to Lexie that I could get up on the top of the cushions just like her, so once I got on the couch, I jumped and jumped and leaped and leaped, but I just couldn't make it to the top. And then I saw something out of the corner of my eye. It was one of those throw pillows that sits at the end of the couch. OK, you probably just see it as a simple throw pillow, but that day I saw "stairs"! One leap onto the throw pillow and another leap to the

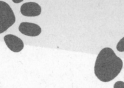

... I learned that it's not a good idea to jump off the couch onto a hard tile floor . . .

YOW!

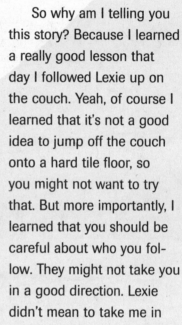

top of the couch, and voila, I made it! Now you might not think that sounds like a big deal, but let me tell you—to a little pup like me, it was like climbing Mount Everest. When I got to the top, I started strutting around like a big show-off to get Lexie's attention. I felt like I was on top of the world. Lexie didn't seem very impressed and just kinda lay there staring at me like I had spinach stuck in my teeth or something. After awhile, Lexie got up and jumped off the couch. I wanted to prove how cool I was, so I followed her . . . right off the top.

All of a sudden, I started yelping in pain! The tile floor was really hard and when I landed on it, my legs just went all wobbly. My parents came running over and scooped me up and rushed me to the vet. The whole time I was really scared, but I tried to be brave. After the vet looked at me, he said I had broken both my front legs. I wasn't really sure what that meant, but the next thing I knew, he was putting these funny-looking green casts on my legs! I had to wear those things for about 8 weeks and it was really hard to walk and I couldn't get them wet. When my mom would take me out on walks, sometimes people would just stare at me and point.

So why am I telling you this story? Because I learned a really good lesson that day I followed Lexie up on the couch. Yeah, of course I learned that it's not a good idea to jump off the couch onto a hard tile floor, so you might not want to try that. But more importantly, I learned that you should be careful about who you follow. They might not take you in a good direction. Lexie didn't mean to take me in the wrong direction, but I made the choice to tag along and try to keep up with her.

For Christians, it's important that we only follow people who are following the Lord. You know, the ones who are really trying to live like God would want them to. Even then, they will sometimes make wrong choices and end up going in the wrong direction. That's why we should try to follow God first and foremost, before following anyone else. I guess that would kind of make us the leaders. Wow, I like the thought of being a leader! I think I'll go take Lexie's chew bone and see if I can get her to follow ME for a change. I bet it'll work!

Follow my example, as I follow the example of Christ. –1 Corinthians 11:1✱

JUST BETWEEN US

Bonus!

Check out pictures of Vicki's dogs, Lexie and Scout, and see what they've been up to lately! Here's how: Have your mom go to vickicourtney.com and click on "blog." When she gets there, have her look in the margin for "Just Between Us," and voila, you're there! This part of Vicki's Web site is just for YOU!

1. Are you more of a leader or a follower?

2. Have you ever followed someone (or copied one of your friends) and learned that it was the wrong direction? If yes, what happened?

3. Before making a decision to do something, how can you make sure it's the choice God would want you to make?

Super-Chick Cooking 101

by Julie Ferwerda

Dreamy Daughter Delights

In a large pot combine the following (except PFMs):

4 c. peeled and diced prayers and devotionals (P&D)

1 lb. disobedience

2 c. whining and complaining

2 c. gripes and arguing

1 bag frozen words and thoughts

2 tablespoons laziness

¼ teaspoon sneaky behavior

Set aside: 1 gallon of "I'm-sorry-please-forgive-mes" (PFMs)

Dreamy Daughter Delights, cont.

Frosting:

3 melted cubes of respect

1 box helpful attitude

1 jumbo package of honesty

1 large handful of responsibility

1 tablespoon humor

Suggestion Sprinkles

Directions: Over high heat, bring all ingredients to a boil. Cook as long as needed until the P&D changes texture of all ingredients into a sweet syrupy consistency, the opposite of how it started. Just before removing from fire, stir in PFMs. Pour into a super-chick cake pan and cool completely before frosting. After frosting, sprinkle with constructive suggestions from mom and dad. Cut into squares and enjoy together!

Super-Chick Cooking 101

by Julie Ferwerda

Better than Brownie BFFs

2 listening ears

2 sealed lips

2 cups understanding

3 lbs. unselfishness

1 diced chunk of loyalty

1 large stalk unconditional love

A generous handful of fun ideas

1 cup creative brain cells

1 gallon of "I'm-sorry-please-forgive-mes" (PFMs)

Dash of salty tears

Directions: Mix all ingredients including tears for sharing in the down times of life together. Form into one massive BFF mound and let set until firm. Mold or roll and cut into fun and creative shapes as desired. When not in use, keep safely protected in special prayer shrink-wrap in a highly accessible location and enjoy for years to come!✽

Quiz

R u a Faithful Friend?

by Susan Jones

Faithfulness is an important characteristic to have in friendship. Just like God is faithful to us, he expects us to be faithful to others. Finish these stories to find out if you're a faithful friend!

ScenaRio #1

You and your best friend _____ are inseparable. You do everything together.
        (name of bf)

From_____ and _____ to _____. One of your
    (fun outside activity)   *(fun inside activity)*   *(fun church activity)*

favorite things to do is listen to _____ together and sing along.
                    (favorite singer/band)

Sometimes you even act as if you're auditioning for _____ and
                        (TV talent contest)

each takes turns trying out. You dreamed about going to see _____ one day. Your mom
                            (favorite singer/band)

knew that you loved _____ and heard that _____ was/were coming to
            (favorite singer/band)   *(he/she/they)*

_____ for a concert. For your birthday, she got you a ticket, plus an extra one to
    (city where you live)

invite a friend. When you open the gift you scream _____.
                            (expressive positive reaction)

Your excitement level is at a _____. Next comes the hard part. Who to invite? For as long as
                (number 1–100)

you can remember, you've always wanted to be friends with _____. She is in
                                (girl's name)

_____ grade, absolutely _____ and super popular. But _____ didn't
(a grade above yours)   *(positive adjective)*   *(same girl)*

really even know you existed. You remember overhearing her tell a friend how much she wanted to see

_____, and think to yourself, *This might be my one chance to be her friend. If I invite*
(favorite singer/band)

_____ *I'll surely be in the popular crowd.* On the other hand, you know that
    (same girl)

_____ would really appreciate it, and you had talked for-ev-er about seeing
    (best friend)

_____ together. After much thinking you decide to call _____ to
(favorite singer/band)   *(name of best friend OR popular girl)*

invite her to the concert.

Who did you call? If you invited your best friend, congratulations! You are a faithful friend. You understand the importance of making decisions that value friendship over popularity.

If you invited the popular girl, you've got some work to do! You have fallen into the temptation of choosing worldly things like popularity or status over genuine friendship. For practice, put yourself in others' shoes and see how your (pretend) decisions would make you feel. Don't despair—God can teach us a lot about how to be faithful! (See "Mud, a Very Faithful Dog" on page 62.)

ScenaRio #2

Your friend from _____ called to invite you over to her house on _____ night
　　　　　　　(sport you play/have tried)　　　　　　　　　　　　　　　　　　　*(weekend night)*

for _____ and a movie. You're _____ because you really like her. You
　　(favorite food)　　　　　　　*(positive expressive adjective)*

tell _____ you'd love to, but have to check with _____ first just to make
　　　(friend)　　　　　　　　　　　　　　　　　　　*(mom or dad)*

sure. With hand over the phone receiver (that's only polite, after all), you shout with all your might to

_____downstairs to get permission, when suddenly, you hear a knock on the door.
　(mom or dad)

It's _____, who lives in your neighborhood! She's the "cool kid" on the
　　　　(girl's name)

block and is dropping by to tell you about a _____ party at her house
　　　　　　　　　　　　　　　　　　　　　(fun type of party)

on _____ night. She's never invited you to anything! You are sooooo
　　　(same weekend night)

_____, and you are just about to accept the invitation when you realize that
(positive expressive adjective)

her party is the same night that _____ invited you over. You decide to tell both
　　　　　　　　　　　　　(name of sports girl)

girls that you'll get back to them. You'd rather go to _____'s house for the
　　　　　　　　　　　　　　　　　　　　　(cool kid's name)

_____ party. You think to yourself, *I could always use the excuse of mom wouldn't let me* or
(fun type of party)

I have something else to do to get out of _____'s invitation. But _____ asked
　　　　　　　　　　　　　　(cool kid's name)　　　　　　*(name of sports girl)*

you first. You think about it for a while and ultimately decide to go to _____'s house.
　　　　　　　　　　　　　　　　　　　　　　　　　　(either cool kid OR sport's girl's name)

Where did you end up?

If you went to sports friend's house, good job! You were faithful to the first invitation you had for the evening. You realize that it's better to honor your friend by not ditching her invitation just because something better came up.

　　If you went to a cool kid's house, think about this. Would you really be able to have fun knowing that you blew off the previous invitation? Sometimes it's easy to find a loophole (or a way out) in situations to make it "OK" to do something we know we shouldn't. For instance, you hadn't exactly committed to sports friend that you'd come over yet, so if you accepted the other invitation really quickly you could honestly say that you had other plans. But your conscience would know that your other friend asked you first. Making decisions like this can set you on a path to give in to those "loopholes" later in life. Start making better choices today! ✳

start making better Choices Today!

by Julie Ferwerda

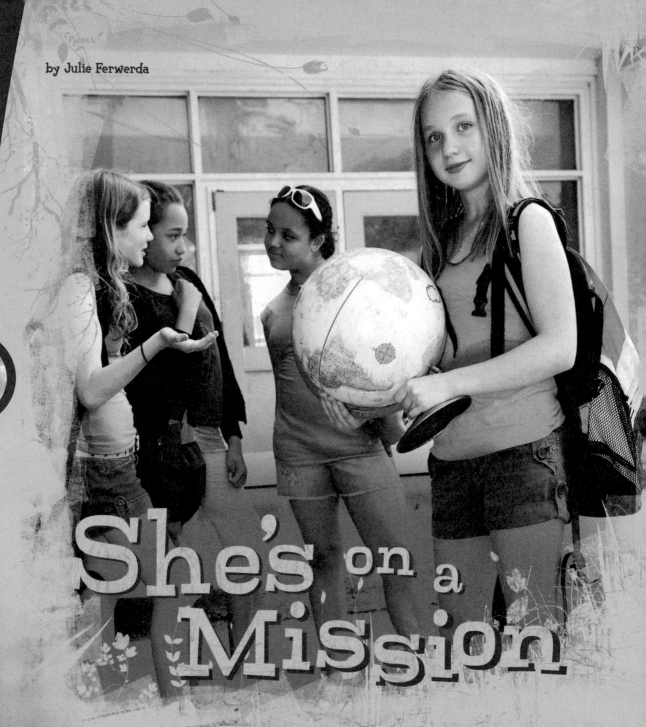

She's on a Mission

Ever wondered what it would be like to go on a mission trip? Would you have to stay in a dark creepy hut with wild critters sneaking in at night? Would your meal options consist of wiggly legs or fuzzy antennae?

Meet Bria. As a twelve-year-old she wanted to do some kind of mission trip, but she wasn't ready for anything too intense for her first experience. Thankfully Bria discovered that there are plenty of options for first-timers that are still fun and adventurous. Check out some of her trip highlights:

Between: Which mission organization did you choose?
Bria: Teen Mania. I heard about them from a friend and decided to try their week-long trip to Tyler, Texas.

Between: What did you do for the week?

Bria: We teamed up with a local church and did something different every day. One day we sorted donated clothes to get them ready to give away. Another day we hung out with little kids from the church day care, playing games and telling Bible stories. We also held outreach activities at parks, so we went door-to-door inviting neighborhood people to come. At the end of the week, we put on a big community picnic where I was able to share my faith with people of all ages.

Between: Did you receive any special training?

Bria: At the beginning we sat down with our leaders and wrote out our testimonies. Then they taught us how to share them without being too pushy, and also how to deal with possible rejection and disappointment. We practiced our testimonies in small groups, which was cool, because it helped us open up more with each other from the start. My testimony even helped a couple of teammates through things they were experiencing at home.

Between: What were your team leaders like?

Bria: Every night our team would break into smaller sharing groups and our leaders were truly interested in what everyone had to say. I'm pretty shy around people I don't know, but they made me feel comfortable speaking up, which helped me make some great friends.

Between: What were the other kids like?

Bria: It was amazing to meet so many other kids that love God. Everyone was so nice and I still keep in touch with some of them.

Between: What was your favorite experience?

Bria: The most special thing to me was helping someone become closer to God, or knowing I helped plant the seed of God in their life. The day I remember most was when a father and his kids came to the park outreach activities and a couple of my friends and I talked to his son about God. At the same time another group was praying with the dad.

Between: Did your life change through this experience?

Bria: God really helped me grow stronger in my attitude toward school and peer pressure. Why let people you'll never see again after a few years influence you to do something that could damage or ruin your life? I met people that helped me see that being the most popular or having the cutest boyfriend doesn't matter in the long run. I learned to fight for what's important and not to let other people stand in my way. Even now, a couple years later, I don't have a boyfriend and it doesn't bother me at all—I'm happy focusing on other things.

Between: Would you go on another trip?

Bria: Yes. I would go to Africa in a heartbeat. ✳

JUST BETWEEN US

1. *Do you know someone who has gone on a mission trip? Who? Where did they go?*

2. *Why do we participate in missions?*

3. *What can you do in your area to join in missions?*

Mission Possible

Interested in missions? Check out these options:

Type: Individual
Ministry: Teen Mania, Garden Valley, Texas
More info: www.globalexpeditions.com
Ages: 11 to 13
Destinations: Texas, Costa Rica, Romania
Length: 1 to 2 weeks
Activities: service projects, evangelism, and kid ministry

Type: Group (bring friends)
Ministry: Group Workcamps, Loveland, Colorado
More info: www.groupworkcamps.com/preteen
Ages: 10 to 12
Destinations: 8 states (Colorado, Minnesota, Montana, Pennsylvania, Tennessee, South Carolina, Virginia, New York)
Length: 5 days
Activities: service projects, kid and various other ministries

Type: Family
Ministry: Praying Pelican Missions
More info: www.prayingpelicanmissions.org
Ages: bring the whole family
Destinations: Belize and Jamaica
Length: You choose
Activities: choose your own—kid ministries, service projects, sports, drama, and more! ✱

You've Got Mail!

by Julie Ferwerda

God's Letters Reveal Hard Core Role Models

There are all kinds of interesting people in the Bible who left an unforgettable mark on the world, and we still talk about them today. Wouldn't it be great if you left that kind of blazing trail? Look up the Scripture and write their names (or descriptions) in the blanks.

1. ____________ This mom gave God her very best.
(1 Samuel 1:22–28)

2. _____ He was a praying man who took care of poor people. (Acts 10:1–5)

3. _____ Radical giving was this person's motto for living. (Mark 12:41–44)

4. _____ He was a loser by the world's standards, but God made him into a winner against an army of millions with the help of only three hundred fellow soldiers. (Judges 7:7–12)

5. _____ This guy's goal in life was to be God's loyal BFF. (Hebrews 11:5)

6. _____ She was an ancestor of Jesus who left a mega-sinful life to join the Israelite CIA (central intelligence agency) when she helped God's spies conquer a city. (James 2:25)

7. _____ A gift worth a whole year's wages wasn't too much dough to spend on the man who had changed her life. He said her extravagant kindness would never be forgotten and might even show up in a tween book someday. (Mark 14:3–9)

8. _____ This guy was both smart and loaded—more than any king ever—because God rewarded him for having the right motives and desires. (1 Kings 4:29–34; 2 Chronicles 1:11–12)

9. _____ This prophetess spent at least fifty years fasting and praying in a temple for the arrival of a certain baby boy. God let her meet that baby before she died. (Luke 2:36–38)

10. _____ She faithfully sat at Jesus' feet when he taught, stayed with him on the day of his death, and was the first to see him when he rose from the dead. (John 19:25; John 20:1–16)

11. _____ When all the odds were against him, this great miracle-performing prophet demonstrated amazing faith and wholehearted devotion to God. (1 Kings 18:16–39)

12. _____ This guy loved God no matter what and always tried to obey him, even when life dealt him a bad hand. God even called him the most moral and good man on earth. (Job 1:8)

13. _____ This king of Judah stayed on God's path and trusted him completely, so God gave him great success in everything he did. (2 Kings 18:5–7)

14. _____ Instead of looking at the giants of their impossible circumstances, these two were the only ones who believed God's opinion instead of what other people thought. As a result, they were moved into a posh new neighborhood with all the bells and whistles. (Numbers 13:30–33; 14:5–9)

15. _____ Making beautiful clothes for poor widows was this godly woman's favorite hobby before she died. Peter brought her back to life after the widows showed him their duds. (Acts 9:36–41) ✳

Answers: 1–Hannah; 2–Cornelius; 3–Poor widow who gave two coins; 4–Gideon; 5–Enoch; 6–Rahab; 7–Woman with perfume; 8–Solomon; 9–Anna; 10–Mary Magdalene; 11–Elijah; 12–Job; 13–Hezekiah; 14–Joshua and Caleb; 15–Dorcas

Buddy Break!

Sweeeeeeet Stuff to Do with Your Buds

by Julie Ferwerda

(P.S. Get permission from Mom and Dad before diving in.)

Take lots of pictures together and make scrapbooks using stickers and markers

Pack a lunch and have a picnic

Write letters in a special journal that you pass back and forth

Open a one-night restaurant (with menus and candles) and cook dinner for your parents/families

Write a silly poem or make up a song

Bake cookies

Go on a discovery expedition in your backyard—look for weird bugs, four leaf clovers, strange plants, etc.

Record yourselves: exchange interviews, perform skits, sing songs, or just be silly

Hold a karaoke contest

Have a craft party (order inexpensive crafts from www.orientaltrading.com)

Organize a one-day sports camp or game day for younger kids in your neighborhood

Make flyers and hire yourselves out to neighbors for house or yard jobs

Cut up (approved) photos into puzzles and then put them together

Start a band

Make up a recipe and cook it together

Blow up balloons, put notes and candy inside, and give them to friends (try it on plastic soda bottles with confetti too)

Make a time capsule (tinyurl.com/33389c)

Camp out in the backyard

Invent a new dance routine to your favorite song

Help an elderly neighbor with house or yard work

Set up a wacky obstacle course and invite friends for a contest

Take turns making up a scavenger hunt for each other with a prize at the end

Recycle cans or bottles for money

Set up a lemonade stand

Organize a family game night

Make a movie with your camcorder

Make a magazine collage

Make your own bubbles (tinyurl.com/2jgn82) and have a contest

Write a pen pal together

Clean out your closet and donate your old stuff to kids who need it more

Draw portraits of each other and hang them on your bedroom wall

Start a collection together

Write a super strange fairy tale with a crazy ending

Redecorate your rooms together

Make up your own holiday and decide how you're going to celebrate it

Make and wrap a present for each other

Hold a spelling bee

Fix each other's hair

Give each other a manicure or pedicure

Play hide and seek

Write a story, taking turns and see where it leads (don't discuss the plot)

Learn some new card games

Put a puzzle together

Invent your own board game

Make small gifts or baked goodies and secretly put them on your neighbors' doorsteps; ring the doorbell and run

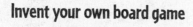

Run through a sprinkler or make a slip n' slide with plastic

Write a play casting your friends and then put it on for your family

Have a paper airplane contest

Subscribe to a magazine and then share

Trade books from your personal library and read together*

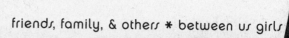

Chapter 5:
just for Fun

talk about
Embarrassing!
by Vicki Courtney

We've all had it happen. No one can escape embarrassing moments. True, some are more embarrassing than others, but everyone has a story about a heart-beating-palm-sweating-cheeks-blushing moment where time stood still and you wanted to curl up and die.

I had an incredibly embarrassing moment happen at a big event where there were lots and lots of Christian authors and singers. I had my teenage daughter with me and we heard that Mandisa (a top eight finalist on American Idol) was going to be there signing her new CD. We had just finished eating dinner and were leaving a restaurant with some of our friends when someone in our group pointed to a lady and said, "Hey look, isn't that Mandisa over there?" She was walking out of the restaurant in front of us and being the awesome Mom that I am, I thought it would be a good idea to catch up with her and get her autograph for my daughter. We were only about 15 feet behind her and I started yelling, "Mandisa!" No answer. "Mandisa!" Still no answer. "Mandisa!" By this time, I had caught up with her and I tapped her on the shoulder and said, "Mandisa, my daughter and I just loved you on *American Idol* and would love to get your autograph."

Vicki, it was so great meeting you!
Mandisa

I'm not usually one to get star-struck, but I couldn't help noticing how beautiful she was in person. She smiled and very graciously said, "I would love to give you my autograph, but there's only one problem. I'm not Mandisa." Now, of course, this probably explains why she never turned around when I was screaming "Mandisa!" I can't remember exactly what I said to her, but I know my face was beet red. I apologized and walked back over to my daughter and my friends, who were laughing their heads off. I'm talking laugh-so-hard-you-almost-wet-your-pants kind of laughing. While they were trying to catch their breath from laughing, I wanted to crawl into a little hole somewhere and never come out.

We may not be able to control those unexpected embarrassing moments, but we can choose how we react to them. In the situation above, I had two choices:

1) I could dwell on it for the rest of the day and beat myself up for being such a dork, or 2) I could laugh my head off and move on with life.

I chose #2 and now, when I think about that embarrassing moment, I crack up. Of course, my daughter never stopped cracking up. She still reminds me about it to this day! And get this, I told the girls in my office about it when I got back and one of them got Mandisa's new book and signed her name on the front and left it on my desk. The note said: "Vicki, it was so great meeting you! Mandisa." When I saw that, I just had to laugh at myself over the whole thing.

The truth is, while the moment may be extremely embarrassing at the time, no one is really dwelling on it as much as you. Within moments, it is usually quickly forgotten. Learn a lesson from me—embarrassing moments are just part of life and you never outgrow them. Oh, and one more word of advice. You might not want to chase down people for their autographs unless you're absolutely sure of who they are! ✳

When you experience an embarrassing moment you can either:

1) dwell on it for the rest of the day and beat yourself up for being such a dork

or . . .

2) laugh your head off and move on with life!

YOUR TURN!
What's YOUR Most Embarrassing Moment?

When I got on stage and didn't know what to sing! —Anne, 11

Sneezing my gum out of my mouth in front of my crush! *—Kaleigh, 10*

Calling 911 on accident! *—Danielle, 11*

My pants ripped in school! —Kristie, 11

I fell over in my chair at school! *—Alex, 10*

I spilled pop on my pants at school. My friend tried to help by soaking them in water, which was super nice, but it made them see-through. She then gave me her Capri pants, but they were two sizes too small, but I had to wear them anyway. —Taylor, 11

When I entered class and smiled with my new braces, and a boy said "Ewww!" —Savannah, 12

I was at a softball game and said, "Get in your ready position, Huskies!" really loud. Then I realized that my team this year was the Wildcats! Oops! —*Izzy, 8*

A bird pooped on my head and I never noticed it until someone at my party noticed. —*Kaelan, 10*

When I blew soda pop out my nose in front of six thirteen-year-olds! —*Elizabeth, 10*

I was talking to my friends while walking and ran into a wooden post. —*Elise, 12*

My crush found out I like him. —*Mikaela, 10*

One time, I got mixed up and called my teacher "Daddy!" —*Allison, 10*

I called my young teacher a Grandma—ugh! —*Karly, 9*

Going to school and finding a pair of underwear in my pants from the dryer! —*Keagan, 10*

I thought someone else was my mom and I hugged her. —*Grace, 8*

In third grade I tried to jump over a trash can in my classroom and instead I fell in it. —*Emma, 9*

10 SUPER COOL THINGS about:

Earth

by Julie Ferwerda

1. The earth weighs 5,972,000,000,000,000,000,000 tons, and a ton weighs 2,000 pounds!

2. It's almost 4,000 miles to the center of Earth.

3. The center of Earth is about 7,000 degrees Kelvin (which equals 13,040.6 degrees Fahrenheit).

4. Gravity is not the same everywhere, so your weight varies in different regions.

5. About 1,000 tons of furniture-covering space dust settles on Earth every year.

6. The spectacular colors in fireworks come from minerals taken from Earth.

7. Ninety-six of the world's highest mountains are in the Asian Himalayas.

8. The giant Saguaro cactus can grow as tall as a six-story building.

9. Certain flowers open and close during the exact same hours every day.

10. In a super-dry desert in Chile, it would take a whole century to fill a coffee cup with rainwater.✱

GRRRR...
What Drives You CRAZY?

by Vicki Courtney

Do you know what a "pet peeve" is? Trust me, it's not the kind of pet you would have curled up at the end of your bed at night. The dictionary defines pet peeve as "a particular or recurring source of irritation." I define it as "that one thing that makes you want to go crazy, ninja when it happens." For me, it's people with bad cell phone manners (thus, the article on pages 38–39). Look, I love my cell phone just as much as the next guy and I can't imagine life without it. But sometimes I want to imagine others without theirs. Especially the guy last week who was on my plane and carried on a loud conversation with someone about his recent surgery. Please, I didn't want to know that—can't it wait until he's in a more private location? I'm sure I speak for the person on the receiving end when I say, "Spare us." Or maybe I started to crack when I entered the ladies restroom, to find yet again someone chatting on her phone. I don't care how important the matter is—please don't call me if there are toilets flushing in the background and a woman in the next stall asking two-year-old little Johnny if he made a "poo in the potty." Bad idea.

So, what about you? Do you have a pet peeve? We asked that question in our survey, and now it's your turn to sound off!

What is something that really bugs you?

First Place goes to:

My brother(s) —Savannah, 12; Emily, 10; Kaleigh, 10; Kristie, 11; Ellie, 9; Allison, 10; Danielle, 11; Molly, 11; Lara, 11½; Allison, 8½; Kennan, 8; Danielle, 9

Second Place goes to:

Nails on a chalkboard —Rachel, 10; Anne, 11; Lauren, 11; Jessica, 8; Zachara, 11; Mikaela, 10; Gia, 9; Emma, 9½; Mileah, 12; Gretchen, 11¾; Joclyn, 11

Third Place goes to:

My sister(s) —Alex, 10; Karly, 9; Victoria, 8; Bethany, 12; Riley, 10; Sarah, 10; Andie, 12½; Saige, 10

Runners-Up:

When people eat with their mouth open —Kayla, 10; Danielle, 11; Stephanie, 11; Lauren, 10; Melissa, 11; Ashton, 10

Smacking gum —Ashley, 9; Breanna, 12; Sarah, 8½; Chloe, 9

Unclosed drawers —Tate, 10

When my teeth grate together, or a fork scraping on a plate —Helen, 12

Smoking —Kristin, 12; Valerie, 9

Clicking nails —Casie, 10

Knuckle-cracking —Elise, 12

A girl named Amanda —Olivia, 9

When people say bad words —Elizabeth, 10

Nail biting —Elise, 10

When people tap on my shoulder —Brooke, 11

An annoying boy at school —Madeline, 10

People taking off their shoes in public —Breanna, 11

When people spit while talking —Alex, 11

When cats brush themselves against your legs —Taylor, 11

When people cuss and scream on the bus —Angela, 12

When people take my stuff without asking —Jenica, 11

People tapping their pencils —Caroline, 9

When friends whisper —Jasmine, 10

Loud screeching noises such as when the dentist scrapes your teeth with sharp utensils —Mayson, 11

People who break promises —Meagan, 10

When people mumble —Kylie, 11

When someone interrupts me when I'm talking —Karon, 11

When people click their pens in class —Breeann, 11

When my brother tries to run into me with his bike —Erin, 9

Bad manners —Rachel, 11

When my sisters scream —Jordyn, 9

My brother burping —Addison, 11

Mosquitoes —Sarah Grace, 10

When people wear mismatched clothes —Katie Rae, 10 *

SURVEY!

What is the ABSOLUTE WEIRDEST PET NAME

you have ever heard
and what kind of pet was it?

Mr. Boofoo, a cat *Ashton, 10*

Mr. Barky Von Schnauzer, a dog
Rachel, 10

Minnie Pearl, a dog
Victoria, 8

Zeus, a dog
Tate, 10

Guppy, a dog
Kennan, 8

Speedy, a turtle
Theresa, 12

Kilia, a dog
Jenica, 11

Kitty, a big dog
Jaimee, 10

Frankenstein, a Chihuahua
Kaleigh, 10

Captain Hook, a dog
Rachel, 11

Macentire, an iguana
Corrie, 11

Billy Bob
Joe Rodeo,
a fish
Kristin, 12

Turtle, a dog
Casie, 10

Mojave, donkey
Alex, 10

Tiny, a huge horse
Elisa, 11

Hawky, a chicken
Valerie, 9

Mr. Wuzzles, a guinea pig
AnnaLee, 10

Chowmanca, a dog
Kaelan, 10

Mr. Fluffers, a dog
Morgan, 11

Gator, the hippo Julia, 11

Billy Bob Joe Bob
Zahara, 11

Mr. Bigglesworth, a rabbit
Hope, 8

Froggie, a frog
Elise, 12

Fru Fru, a dog
Riley, 10

Mr. Beans, a fish
Kristin, 12

Cookie Cutter, a dog
Courtney, 11

Tiny, a Great Dane
Helen, 12

Oozo, a neighbor's cat
Brittani, 11

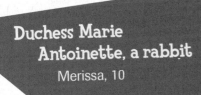

Duchess Marie Antoinette, a rabbit
Merissa, 10

Frank, a fish
Traci, 10

Mr. Fluffy, a cat
Kayla, 10

Lampie, a parrot
(she likes to sit on lamps)
Alex, 11

Borderella, a snake
Mikaela, 10 ✳

SURVEY if you were given

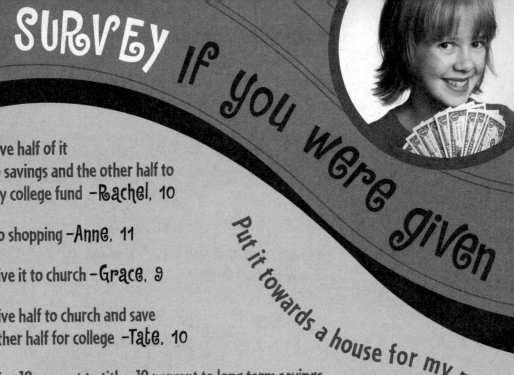

Give half of it
to savings and the other half to
my college fund –Rachel, 10

Go shopping –Anne, 11

Give it to church –Grace, 9

Give half to church and save
other half for college –Tate, 10

Give 10 percent to tithe, 10 percent to long term savings
and the rest to short term savings –Kaelyn, 12

Redo my room and get a bigger mattress
–Kaleigh, 10

Give half to missionaries, and half to bank account
–Emily, 10

Help the homeless –Jessica, 8

Cell phone and iPod –Julie, 11

I would give it all to charity –Victoria, 8

The mall and missions for poor people –Corrie, 11

I would buy myself a new puppy and
save the rest –Kristin, 12

I would donate it to charity
–Elise, 12

Put it toward college –Izzy, 8

Put it towards a house for my mom –Kristie, 11

Go to the mall, buy a horse
–Marissa, 10

$10,000

What would you do with it?

Get a puppy and a cell phone –Laney, 9

I would buy an iPod, donate money to charity and go shopping –Zahara, 11

Give $5,000 to family, $1,000 to charity, and $4,000 to save for college or art school –Bethany, 12

I would move to a huge house and go shopping –Jessica, 9

I would give half to church for an offering, then make a dance studio in my house –Elizabeth, 10

Give $5,000 to charity and save the rest –AnnaLee, 10

I'd buy toys for an orphanage –Melissa, 11

Buy a big trampoline for the back yard and donate to church –Danielle, 11

I would give it to poor people –Grace, 8

I would buy a horse and a ticket to Hawaii –Mileah, 12

I would open up an animal shelter –Emily, 12 *

10
SUPER COOL THINGS *about:*

Animals

by Julie Ferwerda

1. Your dog's sense of smell is 1,000 times more sensitive than yours.

2. Polar bears are always left-handed. (Hey, so is Kermit the Frog.)

3. A pig's tongue has 15,000 taste buds compared to your 9,000.

4. The elephant is the only mammal that can't jump.

5. A giraffe has a 21-inch tongue and can clean his own ears.

6. A python can eat a whole kangaroo or a deer (including antlers) in one bite.

7. Australian termites build mud towers up to 18 feet high.

8. Prairie dogs build miles of underground "towns" that can have up to 1,000 residents.

9. The "Goliath Frog" is the biggest frog in the world and can jump 9 feet high.

10. A dragonfly's eye has 30,000 lenses compared to your one. *